THE

BRITISH ESSAYISTS

WITH

PREFACES

BIOGRAPHICAL, HISTORICAL,

AND CRITICAL

BY THE

REV. LIONEL THOMAS BERGUER

IN FORTY-FIVE VOLUMES

VOL. XIII

LONDON

PRINTED FOR T. AND J. ALLMAN, PRINCES STREET

THE

BRITISH ESSAYISTS;

WITH

PREFACES

2356

BIOGRAPHICAL, HISTORICAL,

AND CRITICAL,

BY THE

REV. LIONEL THOMAS BERGUER,

LATE OF ST. MARY HALL, OXON: FELLOW EXTRAORDINARY OF THE
ROYAL MEDICAL SOCIETY OF EDINBURGH.

IN FORTY-FIVE VOLUMES.

VOL. XLII.

LONDON:

PRINTED FOR T. AND J. ALLMAN, PRINCES STREET,

HANOVER SQUARE:

W. Baynes and Son, Paternoster Row ; A. B. Dulau and Co. Soho Square ;
W. Clarke, New Bond Street ; R. Jennings, Poultry ; J. Hearne, Strand ;
R. Triphook, Old Bond Street ; Westley and Parrish, Strand ; W. Wright,
Fleet Street ; C. Smith, Strand : H. Mozley, Derby : W. Grapel, and
Robinson and Sons, Liverpool : Bell and Bradfute, J. Anderson, jun. and
H. S. Baynes and Co. Edinburgh : M. Keene, and J. Cumming, Dublin.

1823.

G 31122

Printed by J. F. Dove, St. John's Square.

CONTENTS TO VOL. XLII.

No.

BIOGRAPHICAL, Historical, and Critical Preface—Dedication—Preface—Advertisements.

1. Introductory.
2. On the Titles of Miscellaneous Papers.
3. On some Peculiarities in periodical Essays.
4. On the Tendency of the Profession of Letters to promote Interest.
5. On marginal Notes and Quotations.
6. On the personality of poetical Satirists.
7. On modern Songs sung at places of Public Diversion.
8. On the Fallaciousness of History.
9. On Common-place Wit and Humour.
10. On the masculine Dress of Ladies.
11. On the Character of Dr. Johnson, and the Abuse of Biography.
12. On the real and pretended Motives of Writers.
13. On the absurd affectation of Misery.
14. On the Destruction of ancient Mansion Houses.
15. On the Desire of Distinction by living beyond an Income.
16. On the Retirement of Tradesmen and Persons long used to Business and Action, to Rural Life and the Employments of Agriculture.
17. On Xenophon's Memoirs of Socrates, and the Inferiority of Translations to the Originals.
18. On a Species of Injustice in Private Life, in a Letter.
19. On the Rashness of young and adventurous Writers in Medicine.
20. On the Books and fugitive Writings which are proper for the Amusement of small Portions of Leisure.

No.

21. On Imitation of a Model for the Conduct of Life.

22. On Dr. Johnson's Prayers, with a Remark on his Style.

23. On long Prayers, and on the Devotions of Bishop Andrews.

24. On Reading trifling, uninstructive Books, called Summer Reading.

25. On being disgusted with Bashfulness in Boys.

26. On the Effect of ancient and modern Music.

27. On the Effect of Caricaturas exhibited at the Windows of Print-sellers.

28. On modern Heroism.

29. On the Art which has lately been honoured with the Name of Pugilism.

30. On associating with equals for the true Pleasures of Friendship.

31. On the beneficial Effects of the Marine Society.

32. On the Influence of the Professions on the Manners and the Character of the Professors.

33. On the Influence of the medical Profession on the Manners.

34. On the Influence of the Profession of the Law on the Manners.

35. On the Influence of the Military Profession on the Manners, with a general Conclusion on the Subject.

36. On the Amusement of Archery, and other Diversions.

37. On fastidious Conversation.

38. On some of the old Sermon Writers.

39. On the Inconsistences of Avarice, and on petty Avarice.

40. On artful, prostituted, and excessive Praise.

BIOGRAPHICAL, HISTORICAL, AND CRITICAL

PREFACE

TO THE

WINTER EVENINGS.

———

Vicesimus Knox, the author of the following, as well as of other publications, was a native of London, where he was born in the year 1752. He received his education under the affectionate superintendance of his father, who was Master of Merchant-Tailors' School, and had been Fellow of St. John's College, Oxford.

The author of the 'Winter Evenings,' obtained a scholarship, and afterwards a fellowship at the same college. Through the interest of his father with the Merchant-Tailors' Company, Vicesimus Knox was appointed master of Tunbridge-school, which is under the patronage of that opulent corporation. He retained this situation, from the time of his appointment, to the year 1812, when he resigned it in favour of his son, the Reverend Thomas Knox, who is the present master. The publication of his 'Essays, Moral and Literary,' constituted the dawn of his literary celebrity; and, indeed, as far as a taste for the *Belles Lettres* is concerned, that work was never surpassed by any of his subsequent publications. Few works have been better received on their first appearance, than the MORAL and LITERARY ESSAYS of Dr. KNOX. They had a wide and extensive circulation. They were generally read by the old and the young; and obtained no ordinary applause. Some of these ESSAYS, particularly that on the genius and misfortunes of CHATTERTON, were marked by a higher degree of sensibility than the author displayed in any of his later works. Dr. KNOX's character had not much of the glow of genius; but there is more of that vivifying power, or at least the appearance of it, in his early productions, than in those to which he brought the benefit of more mature age, more diversified reading, and more enlarged observation.

In his treatise on 'Liberal Education,' which was published in 1781, Dr. KNOX inserted some severe strictures on the plan of education which was then pursued at Oxford. He exposed the sophistical puerilities that were practised in the *schools*; and shewed how much time was wasted without any increase of knowledge, or any benefit to the understanding. The intrepid freedom, with which the author hazarded his animadversions on these subjects, exposed him to the virulent attacks of those, who were attached to ancient prejudices, or to systems which had reached their natural period of decrepitude; but which were still retained because they were old.

The learned university of Oxford has, however,

since that time, made many innovations upon its ancient modes, and introduced many salutary regulations. All abuses, which are, more or less, connected with existing interests, will, for a time, have their advocates; but the period must arrive, when every fabric, whether civil or ecclesiastical, if it be not opportunely repaired, and accommodated to the improvements of more enlightened times, will sink into contempt, or crumble into dust, without any other active cause than that of its own tendency to dissolution.

The French revolution, which opened a new era of political speculation to the lovers of liberty, commenced when Dr. KNOX was in the vigour of manhood, and in the full maturity of his intellectual faculties. It was much to his honour that he did not, like most of his brethren in the church, shrink back with alarm at the bold theories of government, which were then broached, or conceive a dislike for liberty because the name had been abused, and the spirit outraged, by the frantic excesses of visionaries and enthusiasts. He saw that there was a new, but a salutary fermentation going on in the human mind, by which it would be purified from many of its pollutions; and which would ultimately cause the corruptions of opinion that had been accumulating for ages to disappear.

With the wild and frantic sentiments of those who advocated the crusade against liberty, and caused nearly ten thousand times ten thousand swords to be unsheathed against the rights of man, Dr. KNOX refused to coincide. He felt that this was neither congenial with the spirit of philosophy, nor with the precepts of the gospel. Hence, when during an early period of the late infuriated war, he was invited (in August, 1793) to preach a sermon at Brighton, he had the noble courage to depreciate the military mania of the times, and to extol the gentle and pacific spirit of Christianity, as more favourable to the real interests of mankind. This sermon brought a great deal of odium upon the author at the time, and actually caused him and his family to be insulted at the theatre, by some officers who were quartered in the town. The *terrorism* which prevailed, during the worst periods of the French revolution, has occasionally been displayed, even in this country, in order to excite an unbounded alarm against the cause of political reformation. Those who lived, and lived to reason, between the year 1793 and 1803, must have felt that Mr. PITT's domination was almost as much a reign of terror, as that of DANTON or ROBESPIERRE.

No one can doubt, but that the love of liberty in the bosom of Dr. KNOX, was not merely a transient feeling, but a permanent principle; for he cherished it at the expense of great worldly interests, and not without some danger to his personal security. The work entitled 'The Spirit of Despotism,' which was not till lately generally known to be his production, evinces a higher tone of thought, more fire of sentiment, and more force of expression, than will readily be found in his other works. Indeed, a calmer style was more suited to essays on literary or miscellaneous topics. No work is better calculated than 'the Spirit of Despotism,' to unfold the deformities, and to excite ^a detestation of arbitrary power.

In his religious sentiments, Dr. KNOX appears to have adhered to the doctrine of the orthodox faith, as will be seen by his 'Christian Philosophy,' and his 'Considerations on the nature and efficacy of the Lord's Supper,' of which the first was published in 1775, and the last in 1790. These volumes, indeed, approached the confines of what is improperly termed *Evangelical* Christianity.

The work, entitled 'WINTER EVENINGS,' which is now, for the first time, incorporated with the 'BRITISH ESSAYISTS,' contains a great variety of amusement and instruction. The literary essays will generally be found to evince a mind well stored with learning; and with learning not lying in a state of lumber, but judiciously arranged, and tastefully combined. Dr. KNOX had a nice perception of the beautiful; and, like the best of the Greeks, he united the beautiful with the good. His moral feelings were in strict union with a cultivated taste. His 'WINTER EVENINGS,' in almost every page, furnish ample proofs of a mind that was perpetually labouring to promote a proficiency both in literature and in virtue; and to diffuse a pure and hallowed regard, both for the beautiful and the good.

Dr. KNOX's style is often deficient in strength, but seldom in perspicuity. Where he reasons, he reasons clearly. His diction is rather easy than elaborate; and rather correct than elegant. His periods are not awkwardly constructed, or extended to an unreasonable length. They are, on the contrary, in much the greater number of instances, neat in arrangement, and lucid in sense ; but they have not much fulness of harmony. His mind had not a very large or comprehensive grasp ; but what he knew, he knew sufficiently well to impart to others ; and, if he could not reach to a gigantic height, yet he seldom failed to attain what was within his reach.

In company, Dr. KNOX was rather sedate and retired, than noisy or turbulent. His conversation was not very lively or brilliant. He was one of those scholars, who appear to much more advantage in what they write, than in what they say ; in their books, than in their oral communications. He had never so much fertility of ideas, or promptitude of delivery, as when he had a pen in his hand. Where an author has cultivated the habit of writing more than that of speaking, the tribes of ideas in the mind will not often obey the evocation of any other talisman. The goose-quill thus seems sometimes to exercise a sort of sovereign sway over the brain of the philosopher. If that is the fact, I leave it to the metaphysicians to unravel the mystery.

When Dr. KNOX left his school at Tunbridge, he fixed his residence in the metropolis. He had purchased a commodious house in the Adelphi, and fronting the river. Like most literary men, he found a variety of mental gratification in London, which he could find in no other place.—Indeed in what other place is so much intellectual society to be found ? The author of the 'WINTER EVENINGS,' died in the year 1821. Those, over whose education he so long presided, owe him a monument; and amongst his pupils, or his friends who were most in his confidence, the best critic ought to write his epitaph.

ROBERT FELLOWES, A.M.
Oxon.

died in the year 1801. There is not a single trait in her private life, but was amiable; and among the number of friends who were not in her acquaintance, not one but ought to write the epitaph.

HUMBLY DEDICATED, &c. &c.

TO THE RIGHT HONOURABLE

LORD LOUGHBOROUGH,

LORD HIGH JUSTICE OF HIS COURT OF COMMON PLEAS.

MY LORD.

I AM sensible that there is scarcely any compliment valued in these times than a dedication. To dedicate is commonly but the modest method of extorting patronage. The example is a too common. Favours are frankly paid, and split service. A Dedication is usually regarded or Bookseller than a begger's petition for alms—conveying only flattery and meanness, equivalent to forget even truisms to the King.

But, my Lord, though a Dedication may now be ranked by the public as to which is to address, and may not do that the lieue conceive, but be near as highly agreeable to the Bookseller. In such subject must claim no less to have been considered on a worthy character, and be here spared to Dedicate his own page with the sense of all such men.

I freely confess, that to the small honour, in the able motive of this library I take in this patronage of my book to your Lordship. I feel a pride in presenting, that I consider you to be a worthy subject of the best qualities your heart so highly honoured of his own country ... what, a word, and to act my way. I am an illiterate, my Lord. I am not ...

DEDICATION.

DEDICATION.

TO THE RIGHT HONOURABLE

LLOYD, LORD KENYON,

LORD CHIEF JUSTICE OF THE COURT OF KING'S BENCH.

MY LORD,

I AM sensible that there is scarcely any compliment less valued in these times than a Dedication. To dedicate is certainly not the modern method of obtaining patronage. The avenues to a great man's favour are usually more secret and serpentine. A Dedication is usually regarded as little better than a beggar's petition for eleemosynary relief; and causes stupid opulence to *triumph* over indigent ingenuity.

But, my Lord, though a Dedication may not be valued by the person to whom it is addressed, and may not do him the least honour, yet it may be highly reputable to the Dedicator. It may reflect great credit on him to have fixed his esteem on a worthy character, and to have wished to decorate his first page with the name of an *honest man*.

I freely confess, that to do *myself* honour is the sole motive of the liberty I take, in thus inscribing my book to your Lordship. I feel a pride in proclaiming, that I consider you as an example worthy of the most virtuous times, and peculiarly beneficial, as well as ornamental, in a selfish, a venal, and corrupt age. I am no flatterer, my Lord. I am not

XLII.   B

known to you; nor do I seek to be known. I only
know your Lordship, as I know the Sun, by seeing
the splendour of your public character, and feeling,
in common with others, the beneficial influence of
your public example on society. Why should I flatter?
I have nothing to hope from you, my Lord, but your
esteem; which I value highly, because you have
mine, in your *public character*. I have, indeed, no
pretensions to *this* honour, but those which arise
from a sincere endeavour to promote, in these
amusements of a lettered ease, what I think the
most valuable purposes of society, and what I observe you most anxious to promote, good order,
tranquillity, public spirit, and private virtue. Adu-
lation would be inconsistent with that freedom which
I profess, and would justly forfeit your good opinion. Happily I cannot be suspected of it, when I
thus publicly express my sense of what all men feel
and acknowledge, the high value of a character like
yours, in which *integrity of heart*, and intellectual
ability, appear to be combined. I feel and express
(but it is only in common with the public, who, however divided in other respects, are in this united) a
veneration for one of the best ornaments of the
peerage and of the *tribunal*.

I wish, my Lord, it was in my power to make you
a present less unworthy of your acceptance. You
are certainly able to give the best instruction, and
require not to receive it. Let me not for a moment
be supposed to offer my book to your Lordship, as
containing any admonition of which you can stand
in need; but let me be understood to mean nothing
more by this inscription, than to adorn the first page
by the name of a public personage, an *upright judge*,
whom I conceive to be a living image of those virtues which it is the scope of the book, in a variety
of modes, ultimately to enforce.

In a word, my Lord, I have dedicated the book to your Lordship, that I might have the honour of subscribing myself; I say it not as the formal conclusion of a letter, but that I might have, what I believe to be, the *real* honour of subscribing myself, with profound respect,

My Lord,
An admirer of the *spirit* and integrity,
And your most humble servant,
ANONYMOUS.

PREFACE

TO THE

FIRST AND ANONYMOUS EDITION.

***

However I may be disposed to self-delusion, I am
not so simple as to imagine that a book which has
nothing to recommend itself can be recommended
by a Preface. I think it indeed at once a mean and
vain attempt to deprecate a reader's displeasure by
preliminary submission. The avowal of conscious
defects, of involuntary publication, of youth and in-
experience, and of inability to resist the importunate solicitations of discerning friends, is ever supposed to be insincere; and, if it is true, ought in
many instances to operate in the total suppression
of the work for which it means to apologize. Great
pretensions and bold professions, on the other
hand, justly raise the contempt of a judicious reader.
The liberal spirit of learning should scorn the language of self-commendation, and leave the soft and
flowing diction of puffery to the pulpit of the auc-
tioneer, and the stage of the empiric.

But, though every reader may justly claim a right
to form his own opinion of a book, and will certainly
reject the interference of a party so interested as its
author, yet a Preface is for the most part proper,
since custom causes it to be expected, and the omis-
sion may possibly be considered as the want of a
respectful piece of ceremony. Truly unwilling am
I to be deficient in respect for those, whose good
opinion I must highly value, and for whose indulgence I shall certainly have great occasion.

But to proceed to business without farther preamble, lest I should be thought to write a preface to a preface.

My reader, on taking up his ivory knife to cut open the leaves, may perhaps ask—' What have we here? two new volumes?—And what stupendous discoveries has the author made?—Has he descried a new planet, or fresh volcanoes in the moon?—Has he taught the use of air balloons, and the method of guiding them through the regions of boundless space? —Has he, by beating his brain during the long winter evenings, hit upon the quadrature of the circle, the perpetual motion, the longitude at sea, the northwest passage, the southern continent, the philosopher's stone, or the powder for destroying insects? —Has he exploded the old-fashioned system of morals, and given Christianity the last fatal blow?— Has he proved the lawfulness of polygamy and suicide, and the beneficial effects of private vice on public happiness?—Is the book embellished with capital prints engraved by the very best artists from originals by the painters of the Shakspeare Gallery?—Or is there any delicious abuse of the king, or of the French?—What! nothing of this?—Nothing personal?—Nothing but general remarks on manners and letters?—Then bring the newspaper.'

Indeed, reader, I would venture to say, if I were present, I cannot bring recommendations so valuable as some of these, or so contemptible as others. I will farther confess, that I have no private anecdotes, no public politics, no intrigues, no theatrical history, no lives and adventures of actresses and their poor inamoratos; and that I come to you with nothing but a few plain remarks on men and books made as I travelled along the road of life, with a pocket-book and pencil in my hand, to divert myself on the journey. Such as they are, I submit them to your perusal, hoping that, as a fellow-traveller, you will partake in my amusements with that good humour which will certainly render your journey pleasanter to yourself.

'Amusement,' you say, 'is very desirable; but, as to the amusement of books, the world is already crowded with them.' True, gentle reader; but as my volumes are not very large, there may perhaps be found a little crevice, the world, into which, provided you are really gentle and good-natured, you may find means to squeeze them. If indeed I, an individual in the numerous host of writers, should spare you this trouble, others will certainly supply my place, and you will gain little by partial severity to me. As there is no law that compels a man to read, you may enjoy your repose unmolested whenever you please, only by considering every book which you have no desire to inspect, as so much harmless waste paper.

Indeed, if you are, *bonâ fide*, determined to read none but such authors as Newton, Locke, and Malbranche, far be it from me to interrupt your profound studies, or to pester you with my crudities; but if you are *unus multorum*, and find yourself inclined to send now and then for a book in boards fresh from the booksellers, permit me to be a candidate among the rest for the honour of a leisure hour, while your hair-dresser waits upon you, while you sip your hyson, or while you recline in the corner of your sopha, or your chariot.

Methinks I see you relax your brow, resume your folding-knife, and resolve to look into a volume for a lounge. But why, you ask, this hackneyed miscellaneous form? I answer plainly, because it was the most agreeable to myself; but lest you should think that reason alone too selfish, I add, because I conjectured that it might be the most agreeable to you in the midst of your various studies and more important avocations. I address not my book to systematical and metaphysical doctors, to deep, erudite, and subtile sages, but to those who, without pretending to be among the seven wise men, have no objection to kill a little time, by perusing at their leisure, the pages of a modern volume.

Upon the whole, I comfort myself with the idea, that if I should unfortunately fail to entertain you, I can do you no great injury, which is more than can be predicated of all books without exception. It is far better, in my opinion, to present you with a chip in porridge than a cup of poison.

You observe by this time, and I most readily acknowledge, that I had not much to say for myself worth attending to, in this my preface. Indeed, I entered upon it principally, as I hinted before, to shew that I was unwilling to break in upon you abruptly, and without any ceremony at all. But if the preface answers no other end, it is yet sufficiently useful in affording me an opportunity of declaring, that, though I certainly should not offer you my book, if I thought it quite unworthy of your notice, yet that I am convinced its own merits will not secure it a good reception, without an ample share of your candour. And though I have already acknowleged that I have no great opinion of the propriety or success of such requests; yet, as it can do no harm, I will take the liberty of asking the following little favour: whatever you approve in my book, pray place to my account; but all errors and defects be so kind as attribute to the press, to haste, to inadvertence; or, pardon my freedom, to your own misapprehension; and in so doing you will oblige me greatly.

ADVERTISEMENT

TO THE SECOND EDITION.

THIS book was first published without a name, not from any reluctance to avow the sentiments it contained; but partly from an unwillingness to obtrude a name too frequently on public notice, and partly from a desire to collect the opinions of readers uninfluenced by prepossession, either favourable or unfavourable. But in an age of restless inquiry, an author whose book is so fortunate as to be read, will in vain hope to remain concealed. My secret, unimportant as it was, and though never divulged by me, was soon discovered; and the Winter Evenings were no less confidently attributed to their real author, than if they had borne his name on their title-page.

I have great reason to be well satisfied with their reception. They have had the most honourable testimony in their favour, a very extensive circulation, unaided by the artifices of praise, and the influence of party. Their success has operated as an encouragement to improve and augment them. I have revised all the papers, and added many new ones; to make room for which, some have been obliged to recede from their place.

The division into books and chapters, which I had adopted in imitation of Aulus Gellius, whose *attic nights* first suggested the idea of the Winter Evenings, has been superseded in this edition, because it had the appearance of more formality than such miscellanies require, and was not attended with any peculiar convenience.

These are the principal alterations; and they are

such as, I doubt not, the reader will approve. For *freedom of remark* on all the subjects which have fallen under my consideration, I believe, I need make no apology to the *public at large;* however a few individuals, viewing objects through the prejudices of a party, a profession, a college, or actuated by envy, anger, pride, and personal dislike, may be offended by it. I am unconscious of having written one personal invective; and with respect to the liberty of general censure, a writer cannot deserve to be read, who composes with the shackles of fear about him, armed at all points with selfish caution, and consulting little but his own interest and security. How would such cowardice be treated in the army? and shall it find an asylum in the church, and in the academic cloister!

If I have written freely, I have set my name to what I have written, and am not inclined to shrink from the consequences. I may be traduced by calumny, injured by insidious malice, and insulted by the proud man's contumely; but I can bear it, because I foresaw it. Such is the usual effect of free animadversion.

———Nec rara videmus
Quæ patimur; casus multis hic cognitus—— Juv.

The ingenuity of malevolence against a successful writer, is more prolific in the invention of fiction, than the powers of poetic genius. The lies of an angry detractor are more various than the colours of the prismatic glass, more fantastic in shape than the creations of a poet's eye, which gives to airy nothing a local habitation and a name. To combat them is to beat the air. Though the phantoms rise like the heads of the hydra, time usually destroys them; and to time I leave them.

I know my unreserved manner has raised me many enemies, both public and private; but I also know, and console myself in knowing, that I have not merited their enmity. It has, on the other hand, conciliated some honest friends. The freedom, indeed, of sentiment and expression which gives offence is, I am sure, in itself an honourable quality. Attempts like mine have been, and will always be, partially misunderstood and misrepresented. Success alone, even that share of it which the public, in its candour, has been pleased to allow to my various endeavours, is sufficient to excite the bitter resentment of the dull, the envious, and the disappointed. But I have done my duty to the public, in writing my real sentiments in matters which greatly concern the public; and in writing without that *reserve*, which, though it may promote the secular interest of the writer, militates against truth, honesty, and the liberality of an enlightened, philosophical, and philanthropic nation.

I think it a fortunate lot to live in such a nation; in a nation, whose general characteristic is sincerity; in which ingenuous freedom will be honoured with esteem, and where the unmerited malignity of anonymous slanderers will be compensated by the favour and support of honest-hearted Englishmen, who, above all the narrowness of local and professional prepossessions, honour truth wherever they find it.

London, 1790.

Advertisement to the Third Edition.

In the present Edition, which is the Third, many corrections, and some additions have been made; particularly those papers which appeared in the first, but were displaced in the second to admit new ones, are here restored.

1795.

LUCUBRATIONS,

OR

WINTER EVENINGS.

No. 1—40.

—————————————Seros hyberni ad luminis ignes
Pervigilat.————— Virg.

WINTER EVENINGS.

ILLUSTRATIONS

LIFE AND LETTERS
ILLUSTRATIONS

WINTER EVENINGS.

IN the summer season, the genial temperature of
the air, the beauty of a vivid foliage, and the smiles
of universal nature, allure men from their studious
retirement, and tempt them to roam in the sunshine
their flowery—as flowers fade, and the days are gradually obstructed, and the cold weather causes the
swallow to wing her way to more genial climes, the
butterfly to retire to a warm and safe concealment,
and the leaf to assume the yellow and russet tinge
of autumnal decay, and at length to drop from its
parent branch, the man of sentiment sympathizes
with the scene around him, shrinks under his roof,
and into himself, and seeks that solace which the
sunny hill and the verdant mead no longer afford
him, at the fireside, in the converse of those whom
he loves or esteems, in an elegant and philosophic
solitude, in reading, in writing, and in contem-
plating the productions of art during the repose of
nature, in the fine arts.

In a climate uncertain and inclement like our own,

WINTER EVENINGS,

OR

LUCUBRATIONS

ON

LIFE AND LETTERS.

NUMBER I.

Introductory.—Ev. 1.

IN the summer season, the warm temperature of
the air, the beauty of a vivid foliage, and the smiles
of universal nature, allure men from their studious
retirement, and tempt them to roam in the sunshine
from flower to flower; but when the days are gradually contracted, and the cold weather causes the
swallow to wing her way to more genial climes, the
butterfly to retire to a warm and safe concealment,
and the leaf to assume the yellow and russet tinge
of autumnal decay, and at length to drop from its
parent branch, the man of sentiment sympathizes
with the scene around him, shrinks under his roof,
and into himself; and seeks that solace, which the
sunny hill and the verdant mead no longer afford
him, at the fireside, in the converse of those whom
he loves or esteems; in an elegant and philosophical solitude, in reading, in writing, and in contem-
plating the productions of art during the repose of
nature.

In a climate uncertain and inclement like our own,

c 2

fine weather affords a great pleasure, and he who is not urged to exertion by his wants or passions, seems to acquiesce in it, and to require few other gratifications, besides the enjoyment of it unmolested. The mind is gently lulled by it to a luxurious complacency, and finds contentment in the epicurean pleasure of a perfect inactivity. With a mind at ease, to bask in the sunshine, or to breathe the balsamic gale of a zephyr in the shade, is a satisfaction of the sensual kind, no less delightful than pure.

But when the mind is so well pleased without exertion, it seldom engages in study, or serious reflection, unless stimulated by ambition or necessity; and this obviously suggests a reason why books are much less required as the amusement of summer than of winter.

There seems indeed to be something in the garish splendour of a bright sunshine rather unfavourable to contemplation. One would almost conclude, that the powers of the mind, like vapours, are dissipated in the warm months, and concentrated in the cold. Heat undoubtedly relaxes the body, and causes an inertness which disposes the mind to partake of any diversion which offers itself in the open air, rather than retire to the laborious occupations of recluse study. Cold has a contrary effect; and therefore the winter favours the operations of the mind, and induces it to exert itself with peculiar vigour.

But the length of the evenings in winter, which renders it necessary to find some sedentary and domestic diversion, may also contribute to render reading a more favourite amusement in winter than in summer. Books enable the imagination to create a summer in the midst of frost and snow, and, with the assistance of culinary fire, whose comfortable warmth supplies, round the parlour hearth, the absence of the sun, I believe the winter is considered by few as less pleasurable upon the whole than the season of soft breezes and solar effulgence.

The student shuts the door, while the chill wind whistles round his room, and the rain beats upon the tiles and pavements, stirs his fire, snuffs his candle, throws himself into his elbow-chair, and defies the elements. If he chooses to transport himself to warm climates, to regions delightful as the vale of Tempé, or even to riot in all the enchanting scenes of Elysium, he has only to take a volume from his bookcase, and, with every comfort of ease and safety at home, he can richly feast his capacious imagination.

I do not mean to depreciate the delights of summer; but as in this climate we have a long winter, I think it our interest to find out every consolation which the amusements peculiarly suitable to it can innocently supply, and among these I cannot but consider reading as one of the principal. The mind, the very soul, is deeply interested in this; and whatever touches with the divine particle within us, produces a happiness, or state of enjoyment, equally substantial and refined.

In the metropolis of a rich and luxurious empire, inexhaustible sources of amusement are discovered by the ingenious activity of those who seek their maintenance by exhibiting public spectacles, by supplying music, and by convening assemblies of the young, the gay, the healthy, and the fortunate. Perhaps the evening in London is seldom employed by people of fashion, and their innumerable imitators, in the silent occupation of reading, or in the tranquil society of the domestic circle; but in the country, those who do not devote their attention to cards, find themselves compelled to seek occasional entertainment from the shelves of their book-room; and even in the great city, many from choice, from habit,

from confinement, know no better way of passing
away an hour in a Winter Evening, than by turning
over miscellaneous books addressed to their reason
or their fancy*.

For myself, and let the reader pardon my egotism
on my first introduction, I must acknowledge, that,
though I have no objection to cards in moderation,
I have at the same time no taste for them. They
appear to me too dull and unideal to afford a thinking man, who values his leisure, an adequate return
of amusement for the time they engross. In a rural
retirement, what could I do in the winter evenings,
when no society interrupted, but read or write? I
have done both in a vicissitude pleasant to myself,
and as my inclination or my ideas of propriety suggested. In these employments I have found my
time pass away, not only innocently, but pleasantly;
and most of these lucubrations are literally what
their title insinuates, the produce of the Winter
Evenings. Let me be pardoned, if I have presumed
to hope that some, in the various tribes of mankind,
actuated by an infinite variety of pursuits, might
spend an hour in reading, as I have in writing them,
with at least so much diversion as excludes passion
and vice, and prevents the languor of total inaction.
I shall not presume to censure those who prefer
whist, or the theatre ; but some will prefer a book,
and, in pursuit of variety, may sometimes take up
mine.

As I am convinced that happiness chiefly consists in occupation, I will confess that the amuse-

* Admovit jam Bruma foco te?—Pers.

———Posces librum cum lumine—et
Intendes animum studiis et rebus honestis.—Hor.

Has winter drawn you to the fireside?—You will call for your
books and candles, and apply your mind to liberal studies and
honourable pursuits.

ment of my Winter Evenings has been my principal
design; but if, in the variety of my speculations, I
have been led to treat of topics which at the same
time afford improvement, I shall consider it as so
much clear gain*, and as adding a real value to my
production. Indeed, I am clearly of opinion, that
whoever furnishes an intellectual entertainment,
contributing to fill up those hours which are usually
devoted to relaxation, though he should not approach
with the solemn air of a professed instructor, may
yet add much to public and private advantage. He
may occupy vacant minds, which would otherwise
deviate into vanity and vice from the want of avocation. He may engage those hours which might become burdensome, or be injuriously and disagree-
ably lavished in busy and trifling impertinence.

But are there not books enough already for this
and for almost every other purpose? Is not the
world filled with books, even to satiety? Perhaps
so; but the world is wide, and readers more numerous at present than in any preceding age. Education, both liberal and confined, is more general
than ever, and likely to be still more extensively
diffused.

The English language is the language of a vast
continent of people, greatly increasing in numbers,
and connecting themselves in commercial and all
other engagements with all nations. English literature is of course the literature of America. The
learning of England has long been flowing from the
Thames to the Ganges. The authors of this island
are in great repute all over Europe. So that if
writers can produce works worthy of attention, there
is little reason to fear a paucity of readers.

But granting that books are already too numerous,

---

* Lucro apponam.—Hor.
I shall set it down as clear gain.

yet let it be considered, that a new book will often be read, when an old one, of equal or greater merit, will be neglected. Many old books of great excellence are become scarce, and the great number of modern readers could not so easily be supplied with them, even if they knew them, and valued them, as with the multiplied copies of a new publication. Many books, though they once had a great character, and are still found in libraries and catalogues, are fallen into deserved oblivion, and consequently a vacancy is made by their demise for an ambitious candidate to supply their place.

If new publications were prohibited, there is every reason to believe that a taste for literature among the people would decline. The love of fame and the love of novelty are the great incentives of both writers and readers. The profound scholar might indeed rejoice as he pores over the Bodleian folios, that he was not pestered with new works too superficial to attract his notice; but the liberal merchant, the inquisitive manufacturer, the country gentleman, the various persons who fill the most useful departments in life, without pretending to literature, would find a copious source of pleasure and improvement rescinded. Is the innocent delight and improvement of classes, both numerous and respectable, though not professed *literati*, to be neglected? The erudition which is confined to a few libraries, or locked in the bosom of a few scholars, is of small value to the public at large, and consequently, when viewed with an eye to the general welfare of society, of little estimation. It may be compared to a stagnant pool, large perhaps and deep, but of little utility; while the knowledge which displays itself in popular works may be said to resemble a river, fertilizing, refreshing, and embellishing whole provinces, through which its delightful meanders roll their tide.

Whatever the affected pretenders to depth and solidity of science may urge, new publications will always continue to excite curiosity in a country so intelligent, so inquisitive, so free as Great Britain. In every new attempt, Expectation is on tiptoe to see whether there is not some new improvement; and if she finds not all she promised herself, she usually finds something, or at least has been pleasantly occupied in the inquiry.

But if, with respect to the present pages, it should be asked and answered in the words of the Roman poet,

> Quis leget hæc?—Nemo, Hercule, nemo
> Vel duo, vel nemo.—PERS.

> Who'll read such things as these?—O none will read—
> Or one or two at most.

If this answer should unfortunately be a true one, I may console myself with the reflection, that my lucubrations will not be entirely useless; because manufacturers concerned in the mechanical part of a work must be employed, and the trunkmakers supplied. Why may not one waste one's share of paper, that will otherwise be wasted?

> Stulta est clementia—perituræ parcere chartæ.—JUV.

> To spare the paper—that must else be spoil'd,
> Is foolish clemency.

One advantage will certainly attend the waste occasioned by unfortunate authors, since the consumption of paper contributes greatly to the public revenue.

It is with such affected jocularity that writers endeavour to put a good face on a disappointment, which none, who ever thought it worth while to write, could consider with perfect indifference.

The good opinion of readers cannot but be grateful to writers, whatever, in the pride of their hearts, they may insinuate to the contrary. Some have pretended to find a consolatory recompense for neg-

lect in a false contempt, and by saying with the miser
in Horace,

> Populus me sibilat; at mihi plaudo
> Ipse domi.
>
> The people hiss;—but I myself applaud
> At home.

The philosophy, if there really be any such, which
teaches an utter contempt for the opinion of mankind, is favourable to no beneficial quality, and conduces chiefly to the increase of that silly pride from
which it derives its origin.

Though selfish motives of every kind should be
removed, which is more than in the present state
can often be true; yet, whoever wishes to do good,
and to afford a rational amusement, must wish to be
acceptable, for without pleasing, he will find it difficult to profit.

I will make no pretensions to that superiority
which considers censure and applause with equal
insensibility. I confess I shall derive a sincere satisfaction from being well received by my reader.
The present business of self-introduction may be a
little awkward; but, before we part, I hope to obtain his confidence, and that he will not in any respect be the worse for honouring me with his attention.

Introductory papers have usually been more em-
barrassing to writers than those which succeeded
them. Ceremonies of introduction are seldom pleasant in real life; but to write on one's self and one's
own views and undertakings, however pleasing to
self-love, is apt to cause in the reader a considerable
degree of weariness. Lest I should fairly lull him
to sleep on the very first Winter Evening, which
would be an inauspicious commencement, I think it
would be prudent to wish him good night, and say
no more about it.

I will trespass on his patience but a little longer: I find it good policy, like some of my predecessors, to defend my title from the attacks of witticism by anticipation. I desire therefore to give notice, like Mr. Fitz-Adam in the beginning of the miscellaneous paper called The World, that if any one shall be disposed to say, these Winter Evenings are cold, or dark, or dull, or tedious, that more fire or more light is wanted; the joke will be considered as worn out, that it will not be allowed to pass in currency, but be cried down, like coin too light, and deficient in sterling value.

With respect to my title, which is thus exposed to the shafts of witticism, some title was necessary, and that of Winter Evenings appeared sufficiently distinctive. *Attic* Evenings, which Gellius has anticipated, would have been too ostentatious. It would have led the reader to expect a greater quantity of attic salt than I shall be able to supply, and might have tempted him to say,

> Quid tanto dignum feret hic promissor hiatu?—Hor.

> What will this braggart bring to justify
> This boasting?

I believe it will be best to say no more about the motives which produce these Lucubrations to the public eye. I might indeed talk much of a regard for the public good. But I am of opinion, that *pro bono publico* on the front of the house, or in the beginning of a book, is rather a suspicious circumstance. Indeed, it has been observed, that the motive of any conduct rendered most ostensible often operates with least force, and that the inducement studiously disavowed or concealed is, in the ordinary course of human actions, the real spring and the prime mover. The heart is certainly deceitful, and it is the safest method, if we would neither delude ourselves nor others, not arrogantly to assume any exalted superiority of principle, but to let good motives be evinced by good conduct. Whatever pretences I might make on the present occasion, it might appear perhaps, on a careful analysis, that a great portion of the moving principle consisted of mere vanity and a downright *scribendi cacoethes*. If so, though the infirmity of human nature may be lamented, yet the number of authors excited by similar causes will always keep each other in countenance. And, indeed, why should people be outrageously angry with a vain and a poor writer? A man of a restless activity may, in pursuit of distinction, spend his time much more injuriously to society than in writing a foolish book. It is a consolatory reflection, that a book can neither trouble nor hurt us without our own co-operation.

> Un livre vous deplait?—Qui vous force a lire?—Boileau.
> What! does the book displease?—Pray who compels
> To read it?

NUMBER II.

Of the Titles of miscellaneous Papers.—Ev. 2.

That ancient grammarian, Aulus Gellius, with a delicacy which may be deemed a little too scrupulous, is fearful lest the title of his book, Attic Evenings, should be considered as arrogant or affected, and therefore anxiously takes care to inform his reader, that his lucubrations were so called, solely because they were written in Attica during a winter's residence in that country. He is unwilling to let it be supposed, that he intended to assume the merit of *Attic* elegance or wit, or to allure readers by the artifice of an inviting and ostentatious title.

After making his own apology, he proceeds to censure the affectation of titles assumed in ancient times by the writers of miscellanies; and though his strictures on them are generally just, yet he too severely condemns some, which are not deficient either in a decent humility, or in the propriety of their application.

I think it may afford amusement to the English reader to view some of the inventions of classical authorship in that important part of a work, the fabrication of a Title-page. Many of them have been borrowed and greatly embellished by the moderns, in the hope of attracting notice by the first page; as the innkeeper invites the traveller by a gilded Bacchus, a Tun, and a Bunch of Grapes, and the tempting inscription, 'Good entertainment for man and horse.'

The title of The Muses, as Aulus Gellius informs us, was sometimes given to poetical miscellanies, by which the poet rather arrogantly insinuated that his work was peculiarly favoured by the inspiring Nine. But it was by no means confined to poetry. I believe, indeed, it more frequently occurred in history, where Herodotus had set the example of it, by distinguishing each of his books by the name of a Muse. Some critics acquit Herodotus of the apparent arrogance, and suppose that these elegant appellations were bestowed on his books by his sanguine admirers, in ages long after the writer was no more.

The Graces were the names bestowed on three orations of Æschines, to which the beauty of their language is said to have given them a just claim; but this title must not be imputed to the author's vanity, as it is reasonable to believe that it was the voluntary reward of the reader's approbation.

Sylvæ is one of the most elegant, as well as commonest titles prefixed to the miscellanies of the ancients. The origin of it is the Greek Hyle; and the authors, who first assumed it, modestly intimated by it, that they had collected a store of *timber* or materials, which themselves, or others, might hereafter use in erecting a regular structure. The Sylvæ of Statius are said by the critics to be more valuable than his finished compositions. In imitation of him many modern writers of Latin poetry have entitled the miscellaneous parts of their books, Sylvæ; and our own Ben Jonson, alluding to the ancient title of Sylvæ, denominates some of his smaller works, Underwoods. He entitles his ' observations on men and things,' *Timber;* which must appear unaccountably singular to the unlearned reader, and as in truth not a little pedantic. He adds, in Latin, the following marginal explanation : ' The book is called,' says he, ' Timber, Sylva, Hyle, from the multiplicity and variety of matter which it contains ; for as we commonly call an indefinite number of trees growing together indiscriminately, a wood; so the ancients entitled those of their books, in which little miscellaneous pieces were irregularly arranged, Sylvas, or Timber-trees.'

Quintilian describes the works distinguished by the name of Sylvæ, as struck out with the impulse of a sudden calenture, *subito excussa calore,* and assigns causes for the appellation similar to those which have been already mentioned.

If the name should be differently interpreted, and understood to suggest the pleasantness and variety of a *wood,* abounding with every diversity of foliage, and displaying many a sweet flowret in all the beautiful wildness of nature ; Sylva, the Wood, the Grove, or the Forest, would not be improper titles for a *miscellany,* provided it were of merit enough to answer the expectation of beauty had diversity which such titles might justly raise.

Peplon, or Peplos, the Mantle, was prefixed to works consisting of detached pieces on various subjects. The Peplon, according to the description of Potter, was a white garment without sleeves, embroidered with gold, and representing the exploits of Minerva, particularly in the battles of the Giants against Jupiter; but though this was originally the only subject, it was not retained so exclusively as not to admit the embroidery of other figures which had no relation to it. In process of time the heroes of Athens, after an important victory, were delineated upon it with sumptuous elegance, to be exhibited at the grand festival of Minerva, as an honorary reward of past merit, and an incitement to future. Hence arose the idea of distinguishing with the name Peplon such books or poems as described the achievements of great warriors. Aristotle wrote a poem of this kind, and called it The Peplon. It comprised the lives and death of the most illustrious of his countrymen. Every history concluded with an epitaph of two lines. The loss of the Stagyrite's Peplon is an irreparable injury to the Grecian history, and to polite letters. It may not be improper to add, that when the Greeks expressed their highest approbation of a hero, it was a proverbial saying among them, ' He is worthy of the Peplon.'

But the word was not applied only to the Peplon of Minerva. It signified the external vestment of any dignified lady; and from the description of it, may be imagined to resemble the modern or oriental shawl. The ladies of Greece displayed their singular ingenuity in decorating it with the richest and most picturesque delineations which their manual ingenuity could produce; and the art of the weaver, the dyer, and the engraver, had not then superseded the fine operations of the needle.

The poet therefore, who assumed this title, pro-

D 2

mised his readers every variety of the most vivid
colouring and picturesque imagery. He called them
to view a richly-figured tissue, *a mantle* embroidered
with gold and purple. I should think the title more
properly appropriated to the works of the Sapphos
than of the Aristotles, though Aristotle adopted it.
We have, I believe, many ladies in our own country
who could with equal ease and elegance produce a
Peplon in its literal and figurative sense.

A miscellaneous author of antiquity, who wished
to convey the idea of great exuberance and inexhaustible variety, denominated his work Keras Amal-
theias, or the Horn of Amalthea, which will be more
generally understood if I render it The Cornucopia.
The pretty fable of Jupiter's rewarding Amalthea,
the nurse who fed him with goat's milk in his infancy, by giving her a horn of the goat, from which
she should be able to take whatever she wanted, gave
rise to this title, and to the idea of the Cornucopia,
which is now familiar to the illiterate. As a title it
was too ostentatious, and savoured something of the
vain pretensions of empiricism.

A Hive and a Honeycomb conveyed at once the
idea of industry and taste in the collector, and of
sweetness in the collection. It is obvious to conclude therefore, that the Greek word Kerion would
become the title of miscellaneous books; and if the
books were merely compilations from the works of
others, I can see in it no impropriety. But that a
man should compare his *own* works to *honey*, and
invite his reader by his title to taste of the *luscious
store*, is a degree of self-conceit which may perhaps
justify the censure and contempt of Gellius.

Limon, or the Meadow, was a pleasing title given
by the ancients to works variegated with all the colours of a fertile imagination. It affords the reader
cause to expect flowers richly interspersed; cowslips,

violets, blue-bells; verdure, softness, fragrance, and plenty. I imagine it to have been chiefly applied to poetry. I remember to have seen a small collection of juvenile poems by that polite scholar Sir William Jones, to which he has given the title of Limon, in imitation of those ancients whom he admires with warmth, and imitates with peculiar taste.

To mark their *miscellaneous compositions*, every title which could express a collection of flowers has been adopted both by the ancients and moderns: hence Anthera, Florilegium, Anthologia, Polyanthæa; hence also the Nosegay, the Garland, the Wreath, the Chaplet, and the Festoon.

Lychnus, or the Torch, another title mentioned by Gellius, sufficiently pointed out a book which was to diffuse light; but it falls under the imputation of arrogance, and, like Euremata, Discoveries (which Ben Jonson has adopted), raises our expectations to a dangerous eminence.

Stromateus, or the Carpet, resembles the Peplon. Pinax or Pinakidion, the Picture, conveyed an obvious yet pleasing idea. Pandecte, though chiefly applied to collections of law, extended also to miscellaneous books of polite literature, and seems intended to signify something like the monthly magazines, as the word might be rendered in the modern style, the Universal Repository, or General Receptacle.

Enchiridion, the Manual, or rather the Little Dagger, was a common title to works of small magnitude comprehending things of great moment. In its proper sense it was the small sword, which the soldiers wore constantly at their sides for personal defence against any sudden assault. Applied to a book, it signified a little treatise always at hand, comprehending arguments for occasional defence and constant security. The Enchiridion of Epic-

tetus was a compendium of his philosophy, in a
pocket volume, as a pocket companion, no less
convenient to refute the gainsayers, than a pocket
pistol to repel a thief or assassin, or than a pocket
cordial to exhilarate the spirits upon any occasional
depression.

But enough of ancient titles. If Aulus Gellius
had lived in modern times, I believe he would have
considered the titles which he has stigmatized with
the appellation of *festivitates inscriptionum*, diverting and absurd titles, modest and unassuming in
comparison with some which it would be easy,
though rather invidious, to enumerate in the English language. Popular theology, in the days of the
Puritans exhibited some titular curiosities ; such as,
Crums of Comfort, a Shove, Looking-glasses, Path-
ways, Ladders, Doors, Cordials, Jewels, and many
others, which excite a smile, or would offend modern delicacy. Though most incongruous to the
seriousness of rational divinity they are chiefly prefixed to religious books. I believe the authors were
truly sincere in the doctrines they taught ; but, if
they had intended to ridicule what they reverenced,
they could not have devised a more successful expedient than the drollery of a quaint and ludicrous
title-page.

That works addressed to the illiterate should be
recommended by a pompous title-page, is not wonderful. Their sagacious editors know that vulgar
minds are captivated by bold pretensions and warm
professions in literature as in medicine. Since the
artifice is an innocent one, and succeeds in recommending useful books among those by whom instruction is greatly wanted ; while, at the same time, it is
too apparent to deceive the well-educated and sensible, it deserves not the severity of satire, though it
must of necessity excite some degree of derision.

For splendour and copiousness of panegyrical epithet, no age can produce a parallel to many of the curious titles and commendations printed on the blue covers of works delivered to the expecting world in weekly numbers. Language toils in vain for expressions adequate to the excellence of the compositions, the beauty of the type and paper, and the superb elegance of the copper-plates. Grand, imperial, magnificent, unparalleled, are the beggarly epithets which the editors are compelled to use from the deficiency of language. All this is laughable; but it is found to introduce a Bible, or a System of Geography, or a History of England, into the family of some poor mechanic, who spends, on Saturday, for an improving or entertaining book, that sixpence which might otherwise be lavished in riot and intemperance.

In the higher ranks of literature, I know not that any peculiar affectation in titles is at present observed to prevail. There is, indeed, too much good sense in the age to tolerate either arrogance or affectation in a title-page.

The only rule for the *regulation of a title* is, what common sense suggests, that it should be concise, as descriptive of the contents of the book as conciseness will allow, easy to be pronounced, and easy to be remembered. A title-page may be compared to the portal of an edifice. Who would exhibit the magnificence of Grecian architecture, the fluted column, and the sculptured capital, at the entrance of a cottage? Pliny, who ridicules the *inviting titles*, some of which are already described, concludes with this lively exclamation: *At cum intraveris, Dii, Deæque, quam nihil in medio invenies!* 'But when you shall have accepted the invitation and have entered in, ye gods and goddesses, what a mere nothing you will find in the middle!'

A title may inveigle the unwary; but thinking men and posterity will form their judgments solely from the contents of a book; and if they are valuable, the old adage may be applied to them; 'good wine needs no bush.'

If books of repute have not at present pompous titles derived from Greek and Latin, yet public sights and public places and buildings abound in them.

Pliny and Gellius would perhaps be a little severe on Holophusicon, Eiduraneon, Panorama, Vitropyrix, Microcosm, Lactarium, Rhedarium, and Adelphi. It would not, in this learned age, be surprising to see a barber style himself on the architrave of his peruke warehouse, Phlebotomist, Odontologist, Chiropodist, Pogonotomist, and P. C. A. or Professor of the Cosmetic Art. It is a little affectation of no consequence; and therefore one need not exclaim with the satirist,

——Non possum ferre, Quirites,
Græcam urbem,————

————Romans, I cannot bear
The town thus Greekified.

Indeed, the love of pretty and well-sounding names extends to private life, and displays itself at the font of baptism. The names of Dorothy, Deborah, Abigail, Bridget, Judith, Barbara, Prudence, Charity, Grace, Obedience, have given way to Carolina, Wilhelmina, Charlotta, Emily, Amelia, and Henrietta. Even the good old English Ann, Mary, and Elizabeth, are elegantly converted into Anna, Maria, and Eliza. This great improvement of national taste, which is at present visible in the lowest as well as highest class, is doubtless diffused over the kingdom by sentimental novels, where a Deborah or a Bridget, even if she were of a degree of beauty, understanding, and goodness, approaching to *angelic*, would at first sight strike the imagination as—

a shocking creature! Such is the power of names!
And I will agree, that it is very desirable to have *a
good name,* and I hope to see the Emilies and Hen-
riettas of the present day, deserve *a good name,* by
exceeding in virtue and good housewifery, as well
as in elegance of taste, the Deborahs and the Do-
rothies, the Prudences and the Charities, the Loves
and the Graces, of our great-grandmothers.

NUMBER III.

On some peculiarities in periodical essays.—Ev. 3.

THE physicians call a medicine which contains effi-
cient ingredients in a small volume, and of a pleasant or tolerable taste, an elegant medicine. Moralists, who are the physicians of the mind, have
usually been endeavouring to render their prescrip-
tions palatable by the form of administering them,
and to present their readers with an elegant medicine, a moral cathartic, gilded to please the eye, and
sweetened to soothe the taste.

He who writes on morality usually gives advice;
a free gift, which is the least acceptable of all boun-
ties, as, while it adds to our wisdom, it derogates
from what we value a great deal more, our pride or
self-consequence. The draught is nauseous, though
salubrious; hence the writer endeavours to borrow
something from art, to render it an elegant medicine. He infuses into the phial a little syrup of
sugar, or a comfortable cordial, that the patient may
not make wry faces, or throw it out of the window.

No form in England has been more frequently

chosen for this purpose, than that of diurnal or periodical papers. Doctor Addison, and a few others, eminent in the faculty, made them very agreeable; but *repetatur haustus* has been so frequently put on the labels by succeeding practitioners, that the salutary cordial, the *confectio cardiaca*, though rendered as sweet as syrup, operates at last like a dose of ipecacuanha.

Yet every mode of introducing an air of novelty has been tried by the periodical writers. Allegories, Diaries, Eastern Tales, Little Novels, Letters from Correspondents, Humour, Irony, Argument, and Declamation, have been used to vary the form of conveying periodical instruction. These contrivances were successful, till the repetition of the same modes of diversification caused a nausea.

The Spectator himself talked so much about the dress of the fair sex, that, as tradition informs us, his readers began to be weary, and wished him to take his leave. What his animadversions on tuckers, petticoats, and fans, might effect among our grandmothers, I do not know; but at present all such papers, though they may raise a smile, seem to produce little attention, and no reformation.

But though the modes of conveying instruction may lose their estimation by continual recurrence, yet instruction itself can never be depreciated, if it is founded on the solid basis of experience and sound reason; and perhaps the best method of conveying it, is that which is plainly addressed to the understanding, without any quaint contrivance, or laborious attempt at novelty of form, which too often terminates in a disgusting affectation. In an Eastern tale, for instance, one may be pleased with the language, with the imagery, with the ingenuity of the invention; but as to the moral instruction to be derived from it, it would at present be more agreeable and efficacious, if delivered in plain terms, without those visible and palpable artifices which are now become trite and trivial.

Allegories also are now, from their frequency, more valuable for the diction and splendid figures which the fancy of the writer paints, than for their moral efficacy; which I believe in a lettered age might be better accomplished in a manner less indistinct and operose.

Evident imitation, if unsuccessful, becomes contemptible; and even if it resemble its original, it is still considered, like a good copy of a fine picture, as of very subordinate value, and seldom continues to please long after its first appearance. Diaries of Belles and Beaus, Extraordinary Intelligence, Cross Readings of newspapers, are now worn threadbare. Indeed, every mode of humour, which the Spectator adopted, has been imitated so often as to have lost something of its grace.

But the plain and unaffected manner of uttering ideas and sentiments can never be out of fashion; because it is the very manner which nature requires and common sense adopts. Apparel can never be out of fashion, though the cut of a coat, and the shape of a shoe-buckle, may vary every month. It is the great advantage of adhering to nature in the works of art, that what was once excellent will always be so; what once gave a rational pleasure will continue to give it, like a natural spring, which, though it may not throw its waters into so great a variety of forms as the artificial fountain of the engineer, will continue to supply an exuberant stream, when the scanty canal is exhausted or the machinery destroyed.

Labitur et labetur in omne volubilis ævum.—Hor.

It flows and will for ever flow.

Good sense, expressed in good language, interest-

ing subjects of learning, familiarized to the curious,
or rendered agreeable to the idle, cannot fail of being acceptable in general, though they should appear in the unadorned dress of a direct appeal to the
reason; while, in the imitative garb of preceding
writers, they are in danger of becoming ridiculous
or irksome.

The compound names signed by pretended correspondents to supposititious letters in periodical works
become nauseous by continual imitation. The Spectator has a great number of them, and they were
entertaining enough for once; but who can bear,
without exclaiming, *Ohe jam satis est!* the never-
ceasing iteration of such as Kitty Termagant, Su-
sanna Frost, Ralph Crotchet, Abraham Spy, Mary
Meanwell, Rebecca Nettletop, Eve After-day, which
occur to me in a moment on casually opening a volume of the Spectator? Imitation of things so easily imitable produces only the flat and the vapid. It
is better to communicate the sentiments intended to
be conveyed by these characters and names without
a veil, than with one so transparent and so antiquated, as neither to serve the purpose of a covering nor
of an ornament.

The portraying of characters in Greek and Latin
names, such as Curio, Gelasimus, Belinda, Opsi-
nous, though a very convenient mode of conveying
instruction, begins, from its everlasting use, to be
rather dull. It was at first a lively way of speaking
an author's thoughts in an imaginary character. But
the method is so common, that the natural way of
addressing the reader is now more agreeable and effectual. When fictitious names were first used, the
reader was sometimes, usefully for himself, deceived
into an opinion, that a real character was concealed under the mask; but he now knows, as
well as the author, that it is only an obvious imita-

tive trick, used when invention is at a loss to diversify the discourse.

It is the imitation, for ever repeated, of mere modes of conveying ideas, which renders periodical papers of great merit rather distasteful. Good thoughts delivered in this miscellaneous manner cannot fail of being agreeable, when the reader is not palled with attempts to please him by mere tricks, which he has been so much accustomed to already, as not to be in the least pleased by them, but rather to consider them as impediments to the main business, the discovery of the doctrine, the main scope and opinion of the author.

The insertion of letters from pretended correspondents in miscellaneous papers is a convenient mode of expressing some ideas and characters, which an author could not so well or so probably express in his own person. It may be allowed for its convenience; but, when unnecessary, it ceases at present to please, because the artifice is visible, and no longer leaves the reader in doubt whether the letter comes from a real correspondent, which was originally a useful deception. The reader knows, that he who sends, and he who receives, and comments on the letter, is for the most part the same person; and if he looks at the signature, he may give a shrewd guess what is the subject, as the name is commonly a compound of the epithets or words which describe the character. But I must take care here (for *Cynthius aurem vellit*) not to lay down a law which will operate against myself; for, in the course of these Winter Evenings, I shall sometimes have occasion for a country or a London correspondent, and must solicit the reader's indulgence.

Indeed the whole plan of diurnal essays has been so frequently pursued, as to be in danger of causing that effect which a satiety, even of excellence, is too apt to produce on human nature, one of whose strongest appetites is a desire of novelty.

But if affectation, and too servile an imitation, are avoided, there can be no rational objection to communicating ideas on any subject of morality, learning, science, arts, or taste, in short miscellaneous treatises. Modes may be disgustful, but truth and reason must continue to give satisfaction, whether communicated in the form and under the title of diurnal or periodical essays, or of long, just, and legitimate dissertations.

Dissertations and systems are properly addressed to one kind of readers; but not to all. They are improving and delightful to professed students; while to the general reader, they appear heavy and tedious. *Laudant illa, sed ista legunt.* They praise and admire learned and grave writings, but they read those which are more familiar.

Readers may indeed be subdivided into a thousand different classes; but in a comprehensive division they may be separated into the professional, philosophical, and miscellaneous.

Professional readers, those who read either to qualify for the assumption of a profession, or to regulate the conduct and exercise of one already assumed, require regular and complete treatises, according to Aristotle's description, with a beginning, a middle, and an end. However tedious and dull, they must go through such books as furnish, in any way, stores of professional knowledge. Their reading is a duty. They must proceed in the appointed road, like the stage coach, whether the sky be clear or clouded, and whether the country, and prospects around it, be pleasant or dreary. They must drink at the fountain head, whether the water flow copiously in spontaneous streams, or whether it must be drawn from the well by persevering and painful labour.

Philosophical readers, those whose abilities, opportunities, and ambition, lead them to attempt improvements in science, must also penetrate to the *interiora rerum*, and cut through rocks and mountains, like Hannibal, in ascending the eminences to which they aspire. They are not to be diverted in their progress, by listening, like the shepherd, to the purling of the streamlet and the song of the nightingale, nor by culling the cowslip of the meadows. Their very toil is a delight to them; and they come forth at last Bacons, Boyles, Lockes, and Newtons.

But the *miscellaneous readers* are certainly the most numerous; and, as they form not only a majority, but a very respectable part of mankind, their literary wants are worthy of supply. They consist of all conditions, of the young and the old, the gentleman and the merchant, the soldier, the mariner, the subordinate practitioner in medicine and law, of those who hold places in public offices, even of the philosopher and professor, in their leisure hours; and lastly, though not the least numerous or important, of the *ladies*. A beard was once the mark of a philosopher; but in the present age it is not uncommon to see wisdom and taste united with a fine assemblage of features in the most delicate female face. Such students are not to be sent to dull libraries, to strain their fine eyes over worm-eaten folios larger than their band-boxes.

This being a commercial country, let us suppose the case of a merchant, whose education has been liberal, and whose turn of mind gives him a taste for the pleasure of polite letters. His time is much occupied by the necessary employments of his counting-house. He must write letters, attend the Exchange, and see company; yet he has a love for books, and wishes to spend some time every day in his book room. He goes to his villa in the evening, and remains there a day or two; when some weighty concern calls for all his attention. In a life of business, with little leisure, and with that little liable to interruption, shall he read folios and dry treatises, in the Aristotelian style and regularity? He wishes he could perhaps; but he reads for amusement chiefly, and he requires something which he can read, comprehend in a short time, and relinquish without weariness. What so well adapted as an elegant miscellany? and hence it is that the Spectator, one of the first books calculated for universal use, was universally read in the mercantile classes, and still continues in high estimation.

'The Philosopher teacheth,' says Sir Philip Sydney, 'but he teacheth obscurely, so as the learned only can understand him; that is to say, *he teacheth them that are already taught.*'—For the people, there must be a *popular* philosopher; and he must address them, not like a professor in the dreary schools of an antiquated university, but like Socrates, walking among the people, and familiarizing his doctrines to the understanding and taste of those who are found in the ship, the warehouse, the Exchange, the office, and even the manufactory. Life, at all times, in every part, under every passion and every action, admits of moral philosophy. It is not necessary that there should always be a professor's chair, a pulpit, a school, a formal lecture; since at the table, in the parlour, in the garden, in the fields, there is occasion and opportunity for familiar instruction. A pocket volume, an Enchiridion, or a Manual, accompanies the reader in his walks, in his chariot, in the coffee-house, and in all the haunts of busy man.

Miscellanies indeed of this sort, if any thing but their own utility is necessary to recommend them, are not without the sanction of ancient examples.

All works which bear the title of *Saturæ*, are miscellaneous. What are Seneca's Epistles but moral miscellanies? What are Plutarch's *Opuscula?* What Horace's *Sermones?* None of them systematical treatises but popular essays, highly pleasing and improving to the people at large, for whom they were designed. I could enlarge the list by the Deipnosophists of Athenæus, the Saturnalia of Macrobius, and many works of the grammarians, or professed *literati* of early ages. Nor let the grave and austere despise them as trifling amusements only; for the mind is nourished by variety of food, the *farrago libelli*, like the body by a commixture of fish, flesh, fowl, and vegetables.

If a writer is happy enough to present his reader with good sense, with sound and just reasoning well expressed, his work can never be entirely antiquated; because reason, the internal man, like the external, must always continue the same. Men may be disgusted with the tricks of cookery, and sick of made dishes fancifully seasoned and constantly served up; but substantial food will always be relished by guests whose palates are not vitiated by disease.

That form in which the ideas of a miscellaneous writer can be most clearly and agreeably exhibited, is certainly to be preferred; but every proper ornament of style and method may be judiciously applied, without having recourse to little arts which have lost their grace and power by being so frequently used already, as to be anticipated, and even loathed by the reader, who is apt to yawn over them and exclaim,

Tædet harum quotidianarum formarum.—Ter.

I'm sick of this dull dose of daily trash.

NUMBER IV.

*On the tendency of Letters as a profession to promote
interest.—*Ev. 4.

SIR WILLIAM JONES, whose early acquaintance
with oriental learning and premature accomplishments in all polite letters, promised an uncommon
eminence in the maturer periods of his life, laments,
in one of his last publications, that the profession of
letters, though laborious, leads to little pecuniary
benefit; and that it seldom contributes to elevate, in
the ranks of civil life, either the professor or his family. He therefore takes a tender leave of the be-
loved region of the Muses, and,

———————Desertis Aganippes
Vallibus,— JUV.

The muses vale forsaken,

offers himself a votary of wealth and honour in the
profession of the law. He relinquishes the barren
hill of Parnassus, and seems to be cultivating with
success a richer field.

The first love is not easily forgotten; and Sir
William, amidst his severer studies, still pays great
attention to his old friends the Muses, and the public will probably be gratified with many flowers of
Asiatic growth, selected by his elegant taste.

But what he so feelingly lamented is certainly
true. The finest compositions, the most laborious
works of mere literature, would never have made
him a judge, or raised him one step on the ladder of
ambition. As children admire the peacock's plumage,
and wish to pluck a feather from his tail; so the

great, who have sense enough, admire fine writing, and derive a pleasure which costs them little from the perusal of it. They read, are pleased; they praise, and forget the author. Their interest must be exerted, not to patronise letters, but to pay the tutor of their children at the public expense; or to secure parliamentary votes by bartering for them the cure of souls, or the dignified cushion of some rich cathedral. ‘Such a one,’ say they, ‘is an excellent poet, and I hear the poor man is in narrow circumstances; but really every thing in my gift has been engaged to the members for two or three boroughs, and the minister’s list for prebendaries has been for some time filled with the travelling companions and domestic tutors of several young lords who will have great weight in both houses. I wish I could do something for so ingenious a man; but there is nothing to be done for ourselves in parliament without these sugar-plums to give away. The church indeed furnishes plenty of them, but still they are all engaged, and the hungry mouths seem to multiply faster than the douceurs can be supplied. I most heartily wish Mr. Bayes well, and, if he publishes by subscription, he may set my name down for a copy which he need not send me; but any thing more at present it is out of my power to do for him.’

Thus the writer who perhaps has more ability, and who has certainly been more industrious than many in a lucrative or high political employment, is considered in the light of a mendicant, and even then dismissed to his cell, without reward, to mourn over the ingratitude and venality of the world.

To seek learning and virtue is one thing, and to seek preferment and patronage another. The pursuits are often incompatible; and let not him repine at the want of patronage who has been in his study and among his books, when he should have been, consistently with the pursuit of patronage and preferment, at a levee or a parliamentary election. If he were to write successfully in politics, or to manage a newspaper full of falsehood and virulent calumny, he might get something, when his party should prevail in the grand contest for power and profit. But poetry, history, science, morality, divinity, make no votes in a borough, and add no strength to a party; are every body's business, and for that reason, according to a vulgar remark, to reward them is the care of nobody.

If he had employed his time in engrossing deeds as an attorney, or in posting books as a merchant or banker, or in driving a quill in the East Indies, he might have been by this time a member of parliament by purchase, and then, by voting for a number of years for himself, and talking two or three hours plausibly on the right side for his own interest, have sat down at last with a coronet on his head. As a writer on general literature only, in which all men are concerned, he would still have continued in his garret, though the whole nation should have been improved and entertained by his labours, and future generations may receive from them equal pleasure and advantage.

The lucre of literary works falls chiefly to the lot of the venders of them; and the most eminent writers, who have nothing but what their works bring them, would be likely to starve. There are instances, indeed, of literary drudges, who, undertaking mere compilations and low works of little ingenuity and invention, have gained a livelihood; but a man of genius can never stoop to such employment, unless through mere necessity; and then being in a state of servitude, and unable to choose his own subjects, and the manner of treating them, his spirit evaporates, his fire is damped, and he becomes a mere hireling, seeking gain and disregarding reputation.

Publishing by subscription, in the present state of things, is a species of beggary. A man of that independent spirit which marks great abilities, had rather engage himself in a handicraft employment than crave the subscriptions of those who pretend to despise his book, however valuable, and though they cannot understand it, merely because it has solicited their reluctant contribution. Poverty, and a starving family may urge a man to ask subscriptions in this age, for it is certainly rather less ignominious than housebreaking, and attended with much less hazard to the person. But would not his time, his ability, and his industry, exerted in a counting-house or in a shop, have obtained a better reward for him, with less contumely? All I contend to establish is, that they who study *letters*, as mere *literati*, without a profession, will usually derive from them little to gratify their avarice or ambition. Sir William Jones's doctrine and conduct in relinquishing a life of letters for a life of business, are founded on actual observation of the living world, and the state of things in the present age.

Many contend that there should be certain public rewards appropriated by government to literary merit. I fear they would be bestowed by interest and party either on very moderate, or on no merit; like some of the professorships in the universities; like the Gresham professorships in London; like doctors' degrees; like many sinecures, for which the qualification consists solely in the ability to procure them.

Who in such a case should be the judge and the awarder of the prize? Contemporaries often behold living merit through the false medium either of envy or national prejudice. If a writer were rewarded by one party, another would from that moment exert itself to depreciate his character, his abilities, and his works; so that a man of real modesty and merit, who valued his fame or his peace, would often wish to decline the emolument, which would then fall to some bold and empty pretender. How much envy and detraction have been occasioned by the pensions bestowed upon a few in the present reign? A man who gains an income equal to the best of them in a low trade, thanks nobody but God, and his own industry, for it; but the pensioned, or patronised author, has an everlasting debt of gratitude to pay, is frequently doomed to unmanly submission, and surrounded by enviers who leave nothing unattempted to lessen his happiness and lower his fame.

Then welcome a competent mediocrity, with liberty and peace! Let the man of genius love his muse, and his muse shall reward him with sweet sensations; with pictures and images of beautiful nature, and with a noble generosity of spirit, which can look down with pity, contempt, or total indifference, on patrons who have often as little sense to understand, as liberality to reward him.

Milton was poor and unpatronised, and so was Shakspeare. A miserable pittance bought that poem which is one of the first honours, not only of this nation, but of human nature. But is it not credible, that Milton and Shakspeare had internal delights, a luxury of soul, which is unknown to the dull tribe who are often rewarded with pensions and promotion, and which many patrons, with all their pomp and power, would envy, if they were capable of conceiving the exquisite pleasure?

Let the republic of letters be ever free; and let no bribery and corruption prevail in it. Where patronage interferes, independence is too often destroyed. I except the noble instance of Mr. Dyson's patronage of the poet Akenside.

Writing, it may be said, made Addison a minister of state. It raised Prior to public employment from abject obscurity. Burnet, Somers, Locke, Davenant, Steele, and others, in former days, owed their wealth and elevation to their pen. Their success occasioned such numerous competitors, that they injured each other. The public was often glutted. Patriots or courtiers found other ways to effect their purposes than persuasion and argument, invective or panegyric. The prevalence of corruption rendered the assistance of argument less necessary; but still politics are the best field for writers who mean only to serve their own interest, and to improve their worldly condition.

But no kind of writing in the present age is peculiarly fit for making a fortune. Auctioneers, dancing-masters, quack doctors, dentists, balloonists, actresses, opera dancers, equestrian performers, perfumers, these are they whom the British nation either honours with fame, or rewards with affluence. ' He that can tell his money hath arithmetic enough,' says an old writer; ' he is a geometrician that can measure out a good fortune to himself; a perfect astrologer that can cast the rise and fall of others, and mark their errant motion to his own use. The best optics are to reflect the beams of some great man's favour to shine upon him.'

With respect indeed to employing abilities on general subjects of morals and literature, in which no particular party or sect is interested, one must say, with an ingenious writer,

' Whoever is resolved to employ his hours and his labour in this manner, should consider himself as one who lays out his fortune in mending *the highways*. Many are benefited, and few are obliged. If he escapes obloquy, it is very well.

Triumpho, si licet, latere tecto, abscedere.
To escape with safety is a triumph.

And yet such labours alone usually descend to posterity, and such chiefly produce permanent advantages to the public. Who regards the petty controversies of little sectaries, or even the violent struggles of public statesmen and politicians, after the lapse of half a century?

Happy then are they, who, free from sordid motives, seek excellence without regard to its recompense. They will not be without their reward in the final result of things; and, indeed, their internal satisfaction is more than a recompense for the want of secular emolument and honour.

NUMBER V.

On the Use and Abuse of Marginal Notes and Quotations.—Ev. 5.

THE laborious writers of the last century presented most of their works to the public in bulky folios, with a small letter, a large page, a narrow margin, and a great abundance of notes and citations. It was the literary fashion of the time; but the fashion is so much altered, that though the margins are now usually large enough to admit a greater quantity in notes and quotations than the text itself amounts to, yet you may read works consisting of many volumes without stumbling on a single quotation, or finding the uniformity of the beautiful page violated by one marginal comment. Formerly, as you journeyed through a book, elucidations in the margin attended your progress like lamps by the road side: but now, it may be presumed, books shine like phosphorus, or the glow-worm, with inherent lustre, and require not the assistance of extrinsic illumination.

That I approve of quotations myself is evident from my practice; though I have not been without hints, that books would be more saleable without Latin and Greek; the very sight of which, I am told, is apt to disgust those who have forgotten the attainments of the grammar-school. But if a passage which I have read occurs to my mind while I am writing, down it goes; and I have the consolation, that if it displeases some, it may possibly please others. Of one good effect I am secure: it has pleased myself; and I have honestly confessed, that my own amusement has ever formed a very considerable part of my motives both to write and to transcribe.

But seriously, there appear to be some just objections to the old fashion which crowded the page with passages from various authors, and interrupted the context by references continually occurring even to satiety.

The reader, it may be said, either attends to them, or he does not: if he attends to them, not perhaps being able sufficiently to regard two things at once, he neglects the context for the notes, or, at least, loses that ardour, which he may have contracted in continued uninterrupted reading, and which probably would have contributed more to his improvement than any side-lights derived from the commentary. If he resolves not to attend to them at all, in consequence of his opinion that they may be an impediment to his purpose, they might, so far as he is concerned, have been entirely omitted, and the book would have been a less evil by being of less magnitude.

Notes and quotations are often in languages unknown to the English reader, and then they conduce to no other end but to offend and to mortify him. I have no doubt but that many English books have been injured in their sale and circulation by the Latin and Greek notes with which they abounded. Many persons of good sense and well-informed understanding, do not choose to be reminded, on every page, of their ignorance of ancient languages, and are a little afraid of being asked by their children or others, the meaning of passages which they cannot explain, whatever sense and judgment they possess.

Notes and quotations are often inserted ostentatiously and improperly. Many authors seem to be more anxious in the display of their own attainments, than in convincing or entertaining their readers. A few Greek words, and a little Hebrew, conduce very much to raise the admiration of the ignorant or half-learned, who know not with what ease pompous quotations are made by means of Indexes, Dictionaries, Florilegia, Spicilegia, Eclogæ, and Synopses.

It is, I believe, by no means uncandid to suppose, that quotations have been thus easily and craftily multiplied to swell a volume, and to increase its price. The artifice in this case deserves the indignation of the reader, as it resembles the fraud of the huckster, who, in vending his fruit, makes use of a measure half filled with extraneous matter, or with a false bottom placed in the middle of it. If the context of such writers may be compared to the kernel of the nut, the notes and quotations may be said to resemble the husk, yet, by a preposterous disproportion, the husk often contains a much greater quantity than the kernel. Who can wonder if, in such a case, the disgusted reader throws away both the kernel and the shell?

But though something may be said against notes, quotations, and mottoes, yet more, I believe, may be advanced in their favour. If a reader thinks them of little use, or does not understand them, it is easy to neglect them. It is true that they occupy a space on the page, and increase the size of the volume; but these are inconveniences of little consequence, compared with the pleasure and information which they afford to scholars and attentive readers.

A reader is often referred in the margin to another author who has treated the same subject better or more fully, or in a different style, so as to afford additional information or new amusement.

If the passage be transcribed and inserted in the volume before him, the reader is able to consider it without the trouble of recurring to his library; a pleasant circumstance, which saves both time and trouble, and which, I should think, cannot fail of being agreeable to the indolent student of modern times, who only reads on his sofa over his chocolate, or as he lolls in a carriage, or sits under the hands of the hair-dresser.

It often happens that the quotations constitute the most valuable part of a book, and the reader may then rejoice, that he has not spent his money and time in vain; which, peradventure, he might have done, had the author inserted nothing but his own production.

Though notes, quotations, and mottoes, may be very easily selected and multiplied by means of indexes and dictionaries, yet there is reason to conclude, that a writer who applies them *properly*, must have read, or be capable of reading, the authors from whom they are borrowed; and, in these times of universal authorship, it is some comfort to a reader to know that his author is a little acquainted with ancient learning, and able to drink at the fountains of philosophy. Ignorance may sometimes wear the mask of learning, but not constantly. A shrewd observer will discover it from the awkwardness of the wearer.

The more numerous the ideas which a volume furnishes, the more valuable it is to be considered; as that garden or orchard is the best which abounds in the greatest plenty and variety of fruits and flowers. Some of the fruits and flowers are indeed exotic; but if the flowers are beautiful, sweet-scented, and curious, and the fruit rich and high-flavoured, who can complain but the peevish and discontented? You entered the garden in expectation of the common productions of this climate, and you are agreeably surprised with the magnolia and the pine-apple.

The art of cookery has often been used to illustrate the art of criticism; and though many may prefer plain food, and say,

> Pane egeo, jam pontificum potiore placentis,— Hon.

> Plain bread, I want; than daintiest cakes
> To me more acceptable,

yet the majority will approve a rich cake, heightened and improved with ingredients not necessary to constitute the substance of a cake, because, as the logicians say, they might be present or absent without the loss of the subject *(adesse vel abesse sine subjecti interitu)*; but yet, who could with justice blame the cook for adding plums and sweetmeats? Many have not a taste for such sweet things, it may be said; but while the majority have, and while it is natural, the cook must remain without censure. Let those who like it not, refuse it; but let them not condemn the composition, when their own want of taste is to blame.

While mottoes and quotations are added with judgment, and in a limited length and number, they must be considered as valuable additions or pleasant ornaments; neither would I censure an author for inserting in his works curious and valuable passages which he has met with in his reading, any more than the traveller who adorns his house, his staircase, or parlour, with the productions which he has collected in his voyages; they might indeed be spared; they are not necessary, like the bed, the chairs, and the tables, but, like paintings, they are ornamental and amusing to the fancy, instructive to the understanding, and, in some measure, prove the traveller's authenticity.

But while I approve of judicious mottoes and quotations, I must join in reprobating artful and pedantic writers, who crowd their pages with Greek and Latin, merely to exalt themselves in the eyes of the ignorant, and to gratify their vanity. The affectation and crafty accumulation of second-hand sentences on one side, is no less contemptible than the pride of many superficial authors on the other, who call themselves philosophers, but who scorn to light their tapers at the torches of the ancients; who therefore write volumes without a single Latin or Greek word, confidently relying on the solidity and copiousness of their own doctrines: heroic souls in their own estimation! Some, however, with a detracting voice, will whisper, that the true reason of their totally declining to quote Greek and Latin is, that they understand only their mother tongue.

Quotations have been often misapplied by sceptical and infidel writers for the most dishonourable purposes, to give weight and authority to falsehood in the attack of the received religion. An historian, who has spoiled his book by endeavouring to explode Christianity, has been found guilty, by several ingenious answerers, of misquoting, misrepresenting, and mistranslating passages from ancient authors, whom he endeavoured to compel into his service as auxiliaries. But nothing is to be wondered at in one who admires *Nero* for generosity and humanity.

Quotations can then only be objected to with reason when they exceed in length and number, when they mislead the reader by misapplication, when they are neither illustrative nor ornamental, but inserted solely from the motive of pedantic ostentation, or some other sinister inducement. Objections to them arising from idleness, ignorance, or caprice, deserve no notice. They are justified by reason, and by the example of the greatest authors.

The English reader is usually desirous to see Latin and Greek quotations translated. They often disappoint him; because much of their beauty and force arises from the original language. Queen Caroline commanded Dr. John Clarke to translate the numerous and fine quotations in Wollaston's Religion of Nature: he obeyed the Queen, and the quotations were murdered by royal authority.

NUMBER VI.

On the Personality of Poetical Satirists.—Ev. 6.

MR. POPE has introduced a harmony of verse which however difficult to invent, is imitated with ease. The close of the sense in couplets, and the frequent antitheses in the second line, are features so prominent, that an artist of inferior skill, a mere *faber imus*, is able to copy them, and to preserve a very near resemblance.

His translation of Homer is a treasury of splendid language; and he who has studied it will not find himself at a loss for shining epithets adapted to every occasion. I detract not from his merit; for as the improver of English versification, as the introducer of a brilliant diction unknown before, he has justly obtained universal fame.

But that which is laudable in him as the inventor, cannot entitle his mere imitators to any great applause. They may be called good versifiers and pretty poetasters, but they cannot rank with their master as a poet, or an original improver of versification.

While they exercised their imitative skill on subjects not at all injurious, they might obtain approbation for their excellence, and would certainly escape censure; but the candid, the moderate, and impartial part of mankind have lamented that they have stolen the graces of Pope's versification, to decorate and recommend a kind of satire, abounding in virulent and personal invective, of which the Dunciad afforded but too striking an example.

Some works of this kind have been extolled in the highest terms; but the extravagant applause was, in great measure, the ebullition of that unhappy propensity of the human mind which prompts it to rejoice in seeing elevated merit degraded by defamation. Divest such poems of their PERSONALITY, their *local and temporary allusions*, and how small a portion will remain of real genius to recommed them! they would not be read, notwithstanding their glare of epithet, and their sonorous numbers. The wit is not substantial enough to support itself without personal *invective*.

It is usual with these works to rise to universal fame immediately on publication; to bask, like the ephemera, in the sunshine for a day, and then to fall into irretrievable obscurity. Sudden popularity is like a land flood, which rages for a short time, and then returns into its narrow channel, lost in its original insignificance.

One of the principal arts of their writers is to secure attention by seizing the topic of the hour, by filling their poems with the names of persons who are the subject of conversation at the moment, and by boldly surprising their readers with attacks on characters the most respectable, or at least on persons who, from their important offices, provided they are tolerably decent, ought to be externally respected or exempted from virulent abuse and public obloquy. It is the interest of the community that persons in high stations, whose example is powerful, and whose authority ought to carry weight among all the lower ranks, should not be held out to the vulgar as objects of derision unless they are flagrantly enormous. If they have common failings, or have been guilty of errors merely human, a veil should be thrown over them, for the sake of decorum, and of that beautiful order in society, which conduces to a thousand beneficial purposes.

But a spirit of levelling high characters and rank is one of the distinguishing marks of the present times. Unfortunately for all that is decent, and honourable, and right, it has been found expedient that government, or the ministers of government, should be constantly embarrassed, whether right or wrong, by a public censure. The tools employed by the leaders of indiscriminate and irrational attacks are often such as are only fit for dirty work. Unable to effect any more laudable purpose, they have sometimes been incited to asperse ALL the temporary possessors of office, and its consequent power and emoluments, though confessedly meritorious. Not satisfied with attacking the political persons, they have dared to go farther; to enter into the privacies of family retirement for the sake of degrading honest men, and to spare neither age nor sex in divulging whatever envy and malice may have suggested. The poetical satirist has been called upon as a powerful auxiliary in conducting the levelling engine. Some read and are pleased with verse, who would have overlooked the invective of humble prose. Good versifiers have been found ready to engage in this service, and the most exalted persons in the kingdom have been cruelly hitched in a rhyme, and thrown out to the vulgar to be tossed about by the tongue of infamy.

Every loyal subject, every gentleman, every considerate father of a family, every man of common humanity, is hurt at the cruel and opprobrious treatment which the king, justly deemed the very fountain of honour, has experienced from the hands of rhyming satirists. Exclusively of all *personal* considerations, while this constitution is monarchical, the king should be honoured for the sake of his office, and for the sake of the constitution.

Great pretensions to good humour, mirth, and gaiety, are made by personal satirists; but the pretensions are a veil of gauze. It is easy to see, through the pellucid disguise, the snakes of envy, the horrid features of malice, the yellow tinge of jealousy, and the distortions of disappointment, grinning with a Sardonic smile*.

But as a veil is used, as diversion and pleasantry are promised, and as detraction from illustrious merit is but too agreeable to most men, personal and satirical poems are read, and, like wasps, do much mischief in the short period of their existence.

The pain they give to individuals who are thus burned with a caustic, yet are conscious of having given no provocation, is enough to render the practice odious in the eyes of all who consider duly how much a feeling mind suffers on such occasions, and how little right a dark assassin can have to inflict a punishment without an offence; and to bring a public accusation without coming forward to the public as the accuser.

* Hic nigræ succus Calliginis, hæc est
　Ærugo mera.—Hor.

What the Scripture call the *Gall of Bitterness*, seems to give Horace's idea completely.

The practice is injurious to society, as it tends to discourage the growth of virtue and all honest attempts to be distinguished by merit. Such attempts of necessity render a man conspicuous; and he no sooner becomes so, than he is considered as a proper mark for scorn to shoot at, and for envy to asperse. A man may be afraid to exert himself, when, every step he advances, he is the more in danger of attracting notice, and, consequently, of becoming the mark at which the malevolent may 'bend their bows, and shoot out their arrows, even bitter words.'

What a triumph to villany, profligacy, and ignorance, when virtuous, innocent, and inoffensive, characters are thus singled out for that satire which themselves only can deserve.

This is a grievance which requires the interference of the legislature*. Expostulation is in vain ; and even laws, which might redress it, will not be duly executed, in a country where some degree of licentiousness is unfortunately considered as essential to the existence of civil liberty.

NUMBER VII.

On modern Songs sung at Places of Public Diversion.
Ev. 7.

EVERY scholar knows that Bishop Lowth, in a solemn introduction to his Lectures on Sacred Poetry, has inserted, in the very first place, and as one of the most striking instances of the power of poetry, a Greek

---

* Vim dignam lege regi.—Hor.
A wrong which law should curb.

political ballad, which used to be sung by the Athenian liberty-boys at their festive *symposia*, and by the mob and the ballad-singers in the streets and alleys of that celebrated city.   The Bishop, after citing it at full length, suggests, that if, after the memorable ides of March, such a song had been given by the Tyrannicides of Rome to the common people to be sung in the Suburra and the Forum, it would have been all over with the party and the tyranny of the Cæsars.   This ballad (Harmodion Melos) would, in the opinion of the Prelate, have done more than all the Philippics of Cicero; and yet, though in Greek, it is not better than many a one sung in Cheapside in praise of Wilkes and liberty.   It bears a considerable resemblance to several popular songs written by such poets as Tom D'Urfey and George Alexander Steevens, whom some future lecturer in poetry may call (as the Bishop does Callistratus, the author of his favourite song) ingenious poets and excellent members of the state*.

That the Bishop thought proper to select a trivial ballad to shew the force of poetry, when he was to treat of heaven-inspired poetry, evinces that he deemed ballads capable of producing wonderful effects on the human heart, and therefore of great consequence, and worthy to be ranked with the sublimest strains and even with sacred poetry.

I imagine there must have been a favourite tune to these words, which is now lost past recovery; for among us a popular tune and popular words are generally united: at least the words will seldom be long popular without a favourite tune.   Words scarcely above nonsense have had a fine effect when recommended by favourite sounds; *Lillabullero* is an obvious instance, and many others might be enu-

* Ingeniosos poetas et valdè bonos cives.

LOWTH de Sacrâ Poesi.

merated.   Lord Wharton boasted that he rhymed
the king out of the kingdom by it. 'Hearts of Oak
are our Ships, Hearts of Oak are our Men,' is as
good a composition as that of the old Grecian with
the hard name, and I dare say has contributed to
animate many a poor creature, whose unhappy lot
it was to be *food for powder*.——' Hosier's Ghost,'
' The Vicar of Bray,' and 'Joy to great Cæsar,'
had great weight in the times in which they first
appeared.

But if political songs produce consequences so
important, it is but reasonable to conclude, that
bacchanalian and amorous songs have, in their way,
an influence similar and no less powerful.

Music and poetry are wonderfully efficacious on
the mind when they act separately ; but, when
united, their power is more than doubled. They are,
of necessity, united in songs, and the effect is usually
increased by wine, cheerful conversation, and every
species of convivial joy.

I argue, then, that if political songs have had
such wonderful power as to lead on armies to con-
quest, and to dethrone kings, those songs in which
the joys of love and wine are celebrated, must have
done great execution in private life. It is fair, I
think, to draw such an inference.

I proceed to infer, that it is of great consequence
to the cause of temperance, and all other virtues,
that the poetry of popular songs should be of a good
tendency. For as songs may do great harm, so may
they do great good, under proper regulation.

Perhaps we have not improved in song-writing so
much as in other species of poetry ; for the old
songs are still the best, if we judge by that infallible
criterion, popularity.

But such is the love of novelty, that with a new
tune there must be a new song ; and, unhappily the

composers of the poetry are less excellent in their
art, than the composers of the music. The music is
often delightful, while the verse is merely rhyme,
not only unaccompanied with reason, but destitute
of fancy, harmony, and elegance.

But they who can write neither good sense nor
good poetry, can write licentiously, and give to their
insipid jingle the high seasoning of indelicate double
meanings, or even gross obscenity.

If they descend not to this degradation, they yet
represent the passion of love in language, which,
though mere common-place, renders it very difficult
for ladies of delicacy to sing their songs without the
blush of confusion. Nothing is, indeed, more common than to hear young ladies say, ' The tune is
delightful, but the words are nonsensical. We never
mind the words, we only make use of them to sing
the tune, without giving them a moment's attention.'

The effects of a song ought to arise conjunctly
from the music and the poetry. If the words are
considered as of no consequence and unworthy of
attention, it is evident that much of the pleasure,
perhaps half of it, is entirely lost to the singer and
the hearer. But though the young lady may apologize for singing nonsense, or warm descriptions of
passions which her delicacy must conceal, by saying
she does not mind the words; it may be doubted
whether it is possible to learn a song by memory,
and sing it frequently in company, without giving the
words a very considerable degree of attention. The
ear often corrupts the heart by the intervention of
the lyre.

And I think it probable that indelicate songs have
done almost as much harm by inflaming the imagination, as novels and sentimental letters. I do not
speak of songs grossly indecent; for such are certainly never permitted to lie on the young lady's

harpsichord ; but I speak of those which come out every season at the celebrated places of public amusement. The music is charming, and the words are usually well adapted to the mixed audience of those places, but not always so well to the parlour, the drawing-room, and ladies library.

I propose to the musical ladies, or rather to the music-masters, that whenever a foolish or improper song is set to a pleasing and excellent tune, they would seek some poetical composition of similar metre, and of established reputation, which may be sung to the same tune, without any inconvenience, but on the contrary with great advantage, to the tune, to the morals, to the taste ; and with an addition to the pleasure of all young persons who are educated with care and delicacy.

Where young ladies have a poetical talent, which is common in this age, I should think they could not employ it more agreeably and usefully, than in writing new words to tunes which are accompanied with such as they cannot but disapprove. It would be an additional pleasure to the hearers to have, at the same time, a specimen of the fair performer's skill both in music and in poetry.

I cannot dismiss the subject without expressing a wish that the composers of fashionable songs would take care, for their own sake, that the poetry should be at least inoffensive ; for there are many most pleasing pieces of music rejected by respectable families, and consequently soon lost in obscurity, because the words are such as cannot be sung without causing some degree of pain or exciting a blush. This is not indeed a licentious age in theatrical amusements, nor in song-writing, compared with the reign of the second Charles : but still there is a disguised indecency which prevails in both, and which is probably the more injurious, as the poisoned pill is gilded, and as the dagger is braided with a wreath of myrtle.

But exclusively of moral considerations, every man of taste must wish to see good poetry united with good music.

The best * poets of antiquity wrote the most popular songs. Most of the odes of Horace are love or drinking songs. Anacreon has gained immortality by songs alone. Sappho was a song writer. Even great statesmen, as, for instance, Solon, wrote songs for political purposes with great success.

Many of our best poets also who have obtained the rank of English classics, wrote songs; but who writes for Vauxhall? The best writers of the age need not think it a degrading condescension, when they consider the dignity of music and poetry, and how widely their effects are diffused in this musical age and country.

NUMBER VIII.

On the fallaciousness of History.—Ev. 8.

Ornes ea vehementius quam fortassé sentis. Amori nostro plusculum etiam quin concedat veritas, largiare.

Cic. Epist. 1. Lucceius.

Add a little more embellishment than you perhaps think strictly due. Bestow a little more upon your friendship for me than rigid truth would allow.

Quicquid Græcia mendax
Audet in historia.——— Hor.

Her bold untruths in History's page
Romancing Greece unfolds.———

If you have been an ocular witness to an affray, a fire, or any occurrence in the street, and you see an

* Poetæ melici et lyrici.

account of it in all the newspapers next morning, though they should all pretend to accuracy and minuteness, you would find them all vary in some particulars from each other, and from the truth, yet without the least design to contradict or to deceive; but different reporters of the same facts saw them at different times, or in different lights, with various degrees of attention, and reported them with various degrees of fidelity, according to the variety in their powers of memory, or their talents for description.

In explaining the customs and describing places which they have never seen, there is every reason to believe that most of the historians are unintentionally deceitful. It is seldom that neighbouring nations can know with accuracy each other's most familiar actions, sports, diversions, and places of resort, by written accounts or oral description. Nothing but ocular observation can secure exactness. I was lately much diverted with an article from the great French Encyclopedie, quoted in the notes to Mr. Mason's English Garden. The word to be explained is bowling-green, spelt by the lexicographers *Boulingrin.* ' Boulingrin is a species of parterre,' say they, ' composed of pieces of divided turf, with borders sloping (*en glacis*), and evergreens at the corners and other parts of it. It is mowed *four times* a-year to make the turf finer. The invention of this kind of parterre comes from England, as also its name, which is derived from *boule* round, and *grin,* fine grass or turf. *Boulingrins* are either simple or compound; the simple are all turf without ornament; the compound are cut into compartments of turf, embroidered with knots, mixed with little paths, borders of flowers, yew-trees, and flowering shrubs. Sand also of different colours contributes greatly to their value.'

Such is the French description of a bowling-green sanctioned by the great Encyclopedie.

The celebrated Mr. Sorbiere, furnishes the following materials for an ecclesiastical historian of England, in his famous book of travels among us. He says, ' that our chief clergymen, who have pluralities of benefices, make their grooms their curates ; that our bishops horribly abuse their jurisdiction in their excommunications and impositions ; that they are so haughty, that none of the inferior priests dare to speak to them ; that they rob the church, by letting its leases for thirty years, getting all the money into their own pockets, and *leaving only a small revenue to their successors;* and that England is a country, where no man is afraid of committing simony.'

It would be difficult to obtain an exact history of the events of yesterday ; how much more of these which happened a hundred or a thousand years ago, and in times when the art of manual writing was not common, and men were prone to transmit to posterity by tradition, the dreams of the night, and the imaginations of their idle hours, as real and authentic history.

Those who wrote in the earlier periods, finding a dearth of materials, from the deficiency of written documents, sought in the powers of invention what they could not find in the archives of their country. A book was to be made, and it was to be entertaining. The *terra incognita* was therefore supplied with woods and mountains according to the will of the geographer. Hence the stories of Pigmies and Cranes, Gynocephali, Astromori, Hippopodes, Phannisii, and Troglodytæ.

Herodotus, one of the earliest historians, writes a romance under the name of history, almost as fictitious as Don Quixote de la Mancha, but not nearly so ingenious or entertaining ; yet he is called the

Father of History. He might as justly be called the
Father of Lies. The Chaldean history of Berosus,
and the Egyptian history of Manetho, are deemed
but the forgeries of Annius and Viterbo. Sancho-
niathon's Phœnician history is equally destitute of
credit, if there is any confidence to be placed in the
opinions of Scaliger and Dodwell.

Thus the very foundations on which the splendid
fabric of history is to be erected, are destitute of
solidity. But they are usually strong enough to
support the superstructure; which is too often but
a paper building, a house of cards, pretty and diverting to look at, but of little use and value, when the
entertainment it affords is deducted.

It would be a just description of the greater part
of histories, to say of them, that they are historical
romances, founded sometimes on fact, but capric-
ously related according to the historian's prejudices,
party, or misrepresentation, and fantastically embellished by the false colours of poetry and rhetoric.

Writers of history are often in a dependent state,
and are ready to conceal, or palliate, or exaggerate,
any circumstance or transaction, according to the
wishes of a party, a powerful nobleman, or a king.
The learned pate ducks to the wealthy fool, and the
pen of history is often guided by an illiterate despot.

The histories written by different persons of different parties are known to represent the very same
things and persons as laudable and execrable, god-
like and diabolical at the same time.

There is a well-known historical instance of partiality recorded by Polybius, who was himself also
extremely partial. Fabius and Philinus wrote the
history of the Punic war; Fabius a Roman, and
Philinus a Carthaginian. The Roman extolled his
countrymen, and blamed the Carthaginians in every
thing. The Carthaginian threw all the errors and

defects on the Romans, and triumphed in the superiority of Punic valour, wisdom, and generosity. To whom was credit due? Certainly to neither; and have we no modern Fabii and Philini? Let us read the gazettes of different nations in a state of war.

When I am desirous of knowing real facts stripped of fallacy, I look for them in some *chronological* table; but I read not a popular history. I peruse a popular history, only when I am desirous of being *entertained* by composition, by the charms of style, eloquence, and poetical painting; or of being amused with observing the influence of party, or religious prejudice, on the mind of the writer and his admirers. The real facts are the clay which the popular historian, like a modeller, forms into various shapes, according to his own taste and inclination, some to honour and some to dishonour. To some of it he gives great beauty not its own; some he throws away wantonly or artfully, and the rest he shapes into vulgar utensils; or models them into the deformity of caricature. It is a pleasing pastime to view his work; and men of taste and imagination are much delighted with his ingenuity. Weak and inexperienced persons believe him implicitly; others find real truth in him nearly in the same proportion as silver is found in a great mass of lead, or pearls in oyster-shells.

So little credit is to be given to historians, even in the recital of facts of public notoriety! how much less to their delineation of characters, and descriptions of motives for actions, secret counsels and designs, to which none was a witness but the bosom which entertained them? Yet many historians kindly communicate all. You would think them of the privy-council of all nations; that they possessed the attribute of omniscience, though their intelligence never came from a higher source than an old woman's tale.

Your true, classical historian never feels any difficulties for want of matter. When he finds it not, he makes it. He is a poet in prose. I scarcely need mention those fine speeches in the very best ancient historians, not one syllable of which, except in a very few instances, was ever uttered by the personage to whom it is attributed. Truth gives a faint outline; the historian adds shades and colours, drapery, action, and expression. He lays on the red, the orange, the yellow, the blue, the purple, the violet, the black, and the white*.

Some writers in their attack of Christianity have relied greatly on the representations of historians whose characters were remarkably bad both as men and as writers; who also laboured under the *general* imputation of misrepresenting truth, like every other historiographer. Whatever such writers find against the Christian cause in the most contemptible historians, they bring in triumph, and are ready to sing the song of victory, or cry out *eureka*† with Archimedes. But with all their pretensions to philosophy, they act most unphilosophically in giving implicit credit to wretched annalists, paltry tools of paltry princes, who are known to have fabricated a great part of their stories; and who, when they spoke against Christianity, saw it with the eyes of prejudiced heathens, or envious sophists, too proud to behold with patience a sect flourishing on the ruins of their own fame and dominion.

But it will be asked, whether what I have said against the credibility of history in general, may not be applied to the evangelical history. I answer, that

---

* Græcis historiis plerumque poeticæ similis est licentia.

                                                    QUINTILIAN.

The licence assumed by the Greek historians, resembles the licence of poetry.

† I have made a discovery.

perhaps it might, if the credibility of that history did not chiefly depend on its internal evidence. I never yet saw any external evidence of it which might not admit of controversy; but the internal proofs have a counterpart in every man's bosom, who will faithfully search for it, which gives it incontestable confirmation. The Evangelists and Apostles were fallible men like other historians; but the Spirit of God, which operated on them, and now operates on all true Christians, teaches the humble inquirer to find truth there, and there only, in a state of perfect purity. We may amuse ourselves with tinsel and paste in mere human compositions; but gold and jewels are to be dug for in that mine; and happy they who know how to value them.

I will cite one strong internal evidence of the Gospel History, from the preliminary observations to Macknight's Harmony.

' It is remarkable, that through the whole of their histories, the Evangelists have not passed one encomium upon Jesus, or upon any of his friends, nor thrown out one reflection against his enemies; although much of both kinds might have been, and no doubt would have been done by them, had they been governed either by a spirit of imposture or enthusiasm. Christ's life is not praised in the gospel, his death is not lamented, his friends are not commended, his enemies are not reproached, nor even blamed; but every thing is told naked and unadorned, just as it happened; and all who read are left to judge, and make reflections for themselves; a manner of writing which the historians never would have fallen into, had not their minds been under the guidance of the most sober reason, and deeply impressed with the dignity, importance, and truth of their subject.'

There is then no history in the world so artless as

the evangelical, and none which, from its manner, has so great an appearance of veracity.

But though this is not admitted for a moment by the sceptical writer; yet, at the same time, every passage against Christianity in ancient historians, however suspicious their character, is triumphantly cited by him as a full, a strong, and unanswerable evidence in favour of infidelity.

NUMBER IX.

On Common-place Wit and Humour.—Ev. 9.

> Cui non sit publica vena,
> Qui nihil expositum soleat deducere, nec qui
> Communi feriat carmen triviale monetâ.—Juv.
>
> Stale hacknied jokes shall be no longer borne
> Like worthless halfpence by the vulgar worn.

THE common coin which is constantly in circulation among the lowest of the people, usually contracts a degree of filth, which renders it contemptible to the genteeler and richer orders, many of whom never touch it with their hands, or suffer it to enter their pockets, from a fear of defilement.

There is also a common sort of wit, which from constant use in the mouths of the vulgar, is become polluted. It is indeed, in its trite state, fit for none but the vulgar, and ought, like dirty halfpence and farthings, to be chiefly confined to their intercourse.

The wit I mean, I distinguish by the name of Common-place Wit. It might have been sheer wit in the days of our grandfathers; but is now, from an alteration in manners and customs, either no longer founded on truth and real life, or has quite lost the grace of novelty*. It is as obsolete as fardingales, ruffs, and square-toed shoes. It is worn out, quite threadbare, and ought to be consigned to Monmouth-street and Rosemary-lane.

One of the most common topics of common-place wit, is a jocularity on the lord-mayor and aldermen of London, as great eaters, particularly of custard. It might be true formerly that they were addicted to gluttony, and it may be true now that some among them, like other men, have set up an idol in their belly. But gluttony is not now sufficiently confined to them to justify the perpetual and exclusive jokes on their gormandizing, as if it were their peculiar and inseparable characteristic. Gentlemen of education and patrimonial fortune have often been elected into the court of aldermen; and there is no more reason to suppose them fonder of eating when become magistrates, than when they continued in a private station. In general there is a refinement in the present age, which does not allow men of rank and fortune to place their enjoyment in feeding to excess, though it may teach them to indulge the more agreeable luxury of eating with an elegance of palate.

I have known aldermen of singular abstemiousness, who would sit at tables covered with every dainty, and eat moderately of the plainest food; while hungry *would-be-wits*, who were accidentally invited, indulged in excessive gluttony. Yet the *would-be wits*, used to laugh with a grin of self-complacency at their entertainers (as soon as they were recovered of their own cropsickness), for giving what they were pleased to call an *aldermanic* feast.

* Respicere exemplar vitæ morumque jubebo
  Doctum imitatorem―――― Hor.

  Let imitators truly learned and wise
  Inspect the living manners, as they rise.

The common council and the city companies are
standing topics of jocularity, on account of their
achievements with the knife and fork. As it unavoid-
ably happens that some among them are of low and
vulgar habits, and of mean minds, as well as of mean
origin, a few may be observed to compensate the
poorness of their own tables, by gormandizing at a
public feast, where dainties are presented which they
never tasted before, or where the flavour of every dish
is heightened by that fine seasoner to their palates, a
consciousness that it comes free of cost. This, I say,
may be the case in a few instances; but they are not
striking enough to justify an everlasting repetition of
jokes on the worthy liverymen and common-council
of the city of London.

Even if the jokes were well founded, we have now
had enough of them, and let not us be overfed in
one way, while we are ridiculing excess of food in
another.

But not only the lord-mayor, aldermen, common-
council, and livery, but all the natives, and all the inhabitants of London, supply the witlings with a peren-
nial fountain of jocularity, under the appellation of
Cockneys. Your true Cockney, one who was never
out of the sound of Bow bell, is uncommon in the present age. No persons ramble more than the citizens,
to Bath, Tunbridge, Brighthelmstone, Margate, and
all other places of fashionable resort. Perhaps it
would be better if there were more real Cockneys.
Trade would be better minded, there would be less
folly, extravagance, and ruin, and the Gazette would
not be so crowded with advertisements. But the
Cockney was selected as an object of ridicule some
hundred years ago; and so he must continue, or else
the haberdashers of small wit, and retailers of old
jokes, must become bankrupts for want of stock in
trade.

The professions, indeed, will supply them with many articles in their way, ready cut and dried.

The clergyman, in the ideas of these humorists, is no less fond of good eating and drinking than the alderman; and why should he be? since both of them are only on a level with the rest of mankind in this species of enjoyment, which is natural and necessary, and which, with respect to guilt or innocence, may be deemed a matter of indifference. I imagine that the idea of clergymen's eating to excess might arise from the ancient custom of keeping chaplains at the table of great men, where they fared sumptuously every day, and, perhaps, seemed highly delighted, though even then it was expected of them, that they should retire as soon as the dessert appeared.

But if the joke on the parsons was once a good one, it has now lost all its goodness, because it is stale. The parsons, after all, may console themselves, if the jokers can say no worse of them than that they love pudding. A piece of solid pudding, it must be owned, is in itself a far better thing than such witticism, such salt as has lost its savour.

Those jokes on the clerical profession which relate to formal dress, great wigs, grave faces, and long sermons, are now totally unsupported by the manners and fashions which prevail at present in the ecclesiastical *world*. The race of formal *Spintexts* and solemn *Saygraces* is nearly extinct.

The lawyers afford an abundance of ready-made jokes for little wits; but the jokes are so old that they cease to please, except among the witty fraternity, or among the vulgar.

The profession of physic is, perhaps, the richest mine of wit, which the witlings are able to find. Tie-wig and gold-headed canes are inexhaustible; but the physicians of the present day wear neither. There is the misfortune. The barren joker procures

all his stock from the old stores of deceased witlings of the last century; mere rubbish and lumber,
which would be thrown away, if it were not bought
up and retailed by these second-hand dealers in
cast-off trumpery.

The sects, as well as the professions, suggest a
great deal of common-place jocularity. Presby-
terians and Quakers supply a delectable sort of wit,
which comes at an easy rate, being attended with
no expense of thought nor labour of invention. But
the Presbyterian and Quaker of the last century re-
sembled those of the present but little; and the
shaft of ridicule, which might have adhered to some
of them, would now, in most cases, recoil on the
assailant.

National prejudices are another copious fountain
of petty wit. A Welshman is no sooner mentioned
in the society of jokers, than goats, leeks, and red
herrings occur to his polite imagination. A Scotchman brings to mind the Scotch fiddle, famine, oat-
meal, whiskey, barren land, and want of trees: an
Irishman, potatoes, blunders, bulls: a Frenchman,
soup meagre, wooden shoes, ruffles without shirts,
cowardice: an Englishman, roast beef, honour, honesty, courage, riches, every thing glorious and desirable under the sun.

Many of these vulgar characteristics might originally have some foundation in truth; but when
the same dish is served up with the same sauce from
age to age, who can wonder if the appetite for it
should fail?

And now I mention dishes, what a feast of ready-
dressed wit does a dinner supply? Suppose it a
calf's head; then, Pray do you want any brains?
You have tongue enough already. A hare suggests
the witty idea of being harebrained: a goose is as full
of jokes as of sage and onion. The land of *Ham*

abounds with salt, and I wish there were a grain of the true Attic in it. If you want sauce, you are informed that you are saucy enough already.*

In harmless converse, many levities and follies, which arise from an ebullition of good spirits, and are accompanied with good humour, are not only pardonable, but useful, as they contribute to pass a vacant hour with charming gaiety of heart. But in composition, all common-place wit is insufferable; and yet he who is acquainted with the dramatic writings of the age will recollect, that many comedies, and more farces, depend upon nothing else for their power of affording entertainment. The drollery of comic actors causes them to keep their place on the stage; otherwise it would be impossible to sit at them without yawning or hissing. It would not be difficult to mention both poems and prosaic pieces of a sort of humour, founded entirely on ridicule of the citizen, the clergyman, the lawyer, the doctor, the Presbyterian, the Quaker, the Welshman, the Scotchman, the Irishman, the Frenchman, and not displaying one idea which is not to be numbered in the list of common places. The humour, in its day, was perhaps good; but it is time to relinquish it when it is grown threadbare; and I advise all *would-be wits*, who have no other stock in hand but such as I have described, to get rid of their lumber immediately, and set up with as good a capital as they can raise of common sense; recollecting the proverb, that an ounce of good sense is worth a pound of wit. I will add, that common sense will not only be a more useful, but a more agreeable qualification; for, to people of judgment, nothing is more disgusting than the importunate and impertinent vivacity of a petulant retailer of stale, threadbare, old-fashioned wit and humour.

* Vide Swift's Polite Conversation.

NUMBER X.

On the Masculine Dress of Ladies.—Ev. 10.

GORGON, ICON, et AMAZON !--Propria quæ Maribus.

THE Spectator interfered very much in the (*mundus muliebris*) woman's world. I do not know whether he did not condescend too far, in meddling with the affairs of the toilette, considering that he was capable of enlarging on subjects of a kind so much sublimer and more important. But trifling as dress is, he recollected what Horace says concerning the tendency of trifles to lead to serious evils, and gave it a very considerable share of his attention.

The ladies in his day were not so great readers as in the present; and I always consider his making them and their dress so frequently the subject of his lucubrations, an innocent stratagem to draw their attention to his book, and thus to allure them to the noblest speculations on subjects moral and divine.

But if he really thought the dress of the ladies of great importance, and had lived in the present age, a great part of his papers must have been devoted to the subject.

I think it is easy to collect, from what he has written, that he would have highly disapproved the masculine dress for which the ladies in our times have displayed a singular predilection.

There is something so lovely in feminine softness and delicacy, when free from affectation, and not caused by sickness or infirmity, that they who endeavour to hide those attractive qualities, by assuming the air and dress of a man, must be considered as ignorantly defeating their own intentions to please.

Taste requires a congruity between the internal character and external appearance. The imagination will involuntarily form to itself an idea of such a correspondence; and the lady who appears in a manly dress will at first sight suggest the apprehension of a deficiency of female gentleness and grace. This first idea may be superseded by any one who takes time to consider, that the dress is not, perhaps, the consequence of choice, but merely an innocent compliance with a temporary fashion. Yet as first ideas are in general of great consequence, and not always corrected by second, I should think it wise in the female world, to take care that their dress, which they evidently study with an intention to render themselves agreeable, should not convey a forbidding idea to the most superficial observer.

Silks, linens, cottons, gauzes, and all the stock of the milliner and haberdasher, which I forbear to name, lest I should only display my ignorance, have a beauty, a delicacy, and a softness, characteristic of those whom they were designed to embellish. But broad cloth displays a strength and roughness, which is of a piece with the manly character. Notwithstanding this evident truth, nothing is more common in the present age, than to behold ladies of the utmost elegance dressed in broad cloth externally from top to toe. I do not censure the riding-dress, which pleads convenience in palliation of its masculine appearance: but the riding-dress is lately become both the walking-dress and the domestic dress. The *habit* has introduced the great coat, the surtout, in which a lady, buttoned up with broad metal buttons, appears much like the footman behind her carriage; and indeed when she drives her husband or her lover in his phaeton, she might very easily be mistaken at a distance for his coachman.

‘ But it is a charming, warm, and comfortable

dress, and if the lady and her husband or lover like it, pray what right has any body to object to it?'

I believe it may admit of a doubt whether the men, in general, are pleased with it, any otherwise than as it is the fashion; and as they wish their ladies to be in the fashion, like their coats and carriages, their houses and their chattels. There may indeed be a sort of men who have given up their own manly character, and who yet think there should be a certain quantity of it somewhere in the family, and so are not displeased to see it in their partners; but the generality of men, whatever they may assert in polite submission to their ladies, are naturally attached to them for female graces, and must disapprove in their hearts the least assumption of the masculine character.

However, let the broad cloth be confined to the use of travelling or going out of doors; I will only contend that it should not be worn at the fireside. God and nature have made the sexes distinct for wise purposes, and let not the tailor confound their appearance. Convenience and warmth may plead for the masculine dress on the journey, but that plea loses its force in the domestic circle.

Is there not reason to apprehend that the habitual dress has an influence on the manners? Is it not likely that she who constantly assumes a manly appearance, and a roughness of garb, should likewise display something similar in her behaviour? And may not her behaviour gradually injure her disposition, so that in time she will not only appear less amiable, but may be so? I express myself interrogatively and dubiously, leaving the answers to be made by those who, when they seriously consider, are the best able to decide on points like these.

After all, I am far from certain that dress is of so much consequence as the Spectator seems to consider it. It is indubitable that there are excellent and most amiable women, who follow the fashion in dress wherever she leads, without any apparent evil. Good sense, perhaps, may prevent consequences which would otherwise arise; but a mere aping folly in lower ranks and with lower understandings may suffer from things which in themselves appear innocent or indifferent.

Much of the severity on singular dress or new fashions, to which our eyes have never been accustomed, arises from narrowness of thinking, and from prejudice. So long as dress answers the purpose of a decent covering, and a warm clothing, the ornament of it may be safely left, I think, to the discretion of the female wearer.

Persons in high life, urged by the impulse of that pride which is as strong in low life as in high, will be continually endeavouring to distinguish themselves by external appearance. Those on the next step, quite down to the bottom of the ladder, will always be assuming the appearance of those above them. Fancy and invention are put to the rack to find out new marks unattainable, if possible, by the subordinate classes; and nothing keeps them so long distinguished as something very *outrè*, and apparently ugly and absurd. This accounts for very strange deviations from beautiful simplicity.

The deviations, however, encourage trade, and amuse those who have little to do. Let not the satirist therefore vent his spleen on the ladies' dress, provided they do not confound the different distinctions of sex by assuming the dress of men. I would forbid, by censorial authority, if I had it, all beaver hats and broad cloth, except to such venerable matrons as time has honoured with a beard.

How much is continually said on the subject of head-dresses! It is unfair in *men*, except friseurs, to interfere in that province. The most elegant women, in the most classical times, adorned their heads with ornaments, which raised them so high as to leave it matter of doubt whether the head was a part of the body, or the body a part of the head. The dressing of the hair is called by a Roman poet, the *building of a head*; and the English ladies have scarcely yet equalled the Roman edifices, though the painters of caricature have been outrageously severe upon them.

Moralists may certainly find better employment than that of censuring modes of ornament, which are the natural effects of *female instinct*; if the old Grecian's definition of a woman, of which the Spectator is so fond, be a just one, that she is an animal delighting in finery.

NUMBER XI.

On the Character of Doctor Johnson and the Abuse of Biography.—Ev. 11.

THE illustrious character of Pierre de Corneille, the popular dramatic poet of France, induced those who approached him to expect something in his manners, address, and conversation, above the common level. They were disappointed; and, in a thousand similar instances, a similar disappointment has taken place.

The friends of Corneille, as was natural enough, were uneasy at finding people express their disappointment after an interview with him. They wished him to appear as respectable when near as when at a distance; in a personal intimacy, as in the regions of fame. They took the liberty of mentioning to him his defects, his awkward address, his ungentlemanlike behaviour. Corneille heard the enumeration of his faults with great patience; and, when it was concluded, said, with a smile, and with a just confidence in himself, ' All this may be very true; but, notwithstanding all this, I am still Pierre de Corneille.'

The numberless defects, infirmities, faults, and disagreeable qualities, which the friends of Dr. Johnson have brought to public light, were chiefly what, in less conspicuous men, would be passed over as foibles, or excused as mere peccadillos; and however his enemies may triumph in the exposure, I think he might, if he were alive, imitate Corneille and say, ' Notwithstanding all this, I am still Samuel Johnson.'

Few men could stand so fiery a trial as he has done. His gold has been put into the furnace, and, considering the violence of the fire, and the frequent repetition of the process, the quantity of dross and alloy is inconsiderable. Let him be considered not absolutely but comparatively: and let those who are disgusted with him, ask themselves, whether their own characters, or those they most admire, would not exhibit some deformity, if they were to be analyzed with a minute and anxious curiosity. The private conversation of Johnson, the caprice of momentary ill-humour, the weakness of disease, the common infirmities of human nature, have been presented to the public, without those alleviating circumstances which probably attended them. And where is the man that has not foibles, weaknesses, follies, and defects of some kind? And where is the man that has greater virtues, greater abilities, more useful labours, to put into the opposite scale against his defects than Dr. Johnson?

Biography is every day descending from its dignity. Instead of an instructive recital, it is becoming an instrument to the mere gratification of an impertinent, not to say a malignant, curiosity. There are certain foibles and weaknesses which should be shut up in the coffin with the poor relics of fallen humanity. Wherever the greater part of a character is *shining*, the *few blemishes* should be covered with the pall.

I am apprehensive that the custom of exposing the nakedness of eminent men to every eye, will have an unfavourable influence on virtue. It may teach men to fear celebrity; and, by extinguishing the desire of fame and posthumous glory, destroy one powerful motive to excellence.

I think there is reason to fear lest the moral writings of Johnson should lose something of their effect by this unfortunate degradation. To prevent so mischievous a consequence of his friends communications, I wish his readers to consider the old saying, 'that no man is wise at all times;' and to reflect that reason and argument do not lose any thing of their value from the errors and foibles of a writer's conduct. Let them also remember the old complaint, that many see and approve the better part, while from the violence of passion they pursue the worse.

Is it to be believed that the greatest men in all history would have appeared almost uniformly great, if the taste of their age, and the communicative disposition of their intimate friends had published their private conversation, the secrets of their closets, and of their chambers?

It was usual to write the lives of great men *con amore*, with affection for them, and there ran a vein of panegyric with the narrative. Writer and reader agreed in loving the character, and the reader's love was increased and confirmed by the writer's representation. An ardour of imitation was thus excited, and the hero of the story placed, without one dissenting voice, in some honourable nich in the temple of Fame. But this biographical anatomy, in minutely dissecting parts, destroys the beauty of the whole; just as in cutting up the most comely body, many loathsome objects are presented to the eye, and the beautiful form is utterly disfigured.

It is said indeed that not only truth, but the whole truth, should be published and left naked for the contemplation of mankind; for as the anatomy of the body contributes to the benefit of human nature, by promoting medical and chirurgical knowledge; so the dissection of characters tends to the developement of error, which, by being thus exposed, may be avoided.

From such an exposure some advantage may be derived to the philosopher; but I fear little to the multitude. I am rather induced to believe, that the abasement of great characters, and the exposure of defects, prevent the salutary operation of their good example, and of their writings. The common reader seldom makes refined and philosophical observation. But he says, if such men, so learned, so great, so celebrated, were guilty of this failing, or remarkable for that misconduct, how can I attempt, with hope of success, to avoid it? He gives up the contest, and shelters his surrender under the name and authority of the defunct philosopher, whom he once admired, and, while he admired, endeavoured to imitate.

I think it was Egypt in which a tribunal was established to sit in judgment on the departed. Johnson has been tried with as accurate an investigation of circumstances as if he had been judicially arraigned on the banks of the Nile.

It does not appear that the witnesses were partial. The sentence of the public, according to their testimony, has rather lowered him; but time will replace him where he was, and where he ought to be, not-

withstanding all his errors and infirmities, high in
the ranks of Fame. Posterity will forgive his roughness of manner, his apparent superstition, his mis-
takes in making his will, his prejudices against
Whigs and the Scotch, and will remember his Dic-
tionary, his moral writings, his biography, his manly
vigour of thought, his piety, and his charity. They
will make allowances for morbid melancholy; for a
life, a great part of which was spent in extreme indi-
gence and labour, and the rest, by a sudden transi-
tion, in the midst of affluence, flattery, obsequiousness, submission, and universal renown.

The number of writers who have discussed the
life, character, and writings, of Johnson, is alone
sufficient to evince that the public feels him to be a
great man, and it will not be easy to write him down
through mistaken friendship or declared enmity.
He was indeed a great man; but mortal man, however well he may deserve the epithet, Great, comparatively, is absolutely, but a little being; and the
example of Johnson is an additional proof of this obvious, but humiliating conclusion. I wish, neverthe-
less, that his life had been written in the manner of
the French *Eloges*, and with the affection and reverence due to supereminent merit.

Many of his apparent friends, one may suppose,
were of those who forced themselves into his company and acquaintance in order to gain credit, and
gratify their own vanity. They seem to have had
little cordiality for him, and no objection to lower
his fame, if they could raise their own names to eminence on the ruins. Many of them had, perhaps,
been hurt by his freedom of rebuke, and were glad
to gratify revenge when retaliation was out of his
power. If he were alive, he would crush the swarms
of insects that have attacked his character, and,
with one sarcastic blow, flap them into nonexistence.

NUMBER XII.

On the real and pretended Motives of Writers.
Ev. 12.

REAL diamonds and gold are rare, concealed under the earth, or in the beds of rivers; but perhaps truth, as it is more valuable than diamonds and gold, is also more difficult to be found in a state of perfect and unsullied purity. A man scarcely knows the truth of his own mind, his own avowed and professed sentiments : so just is the remark of the Scriptures, ' that the heart is deceitful above all things, who can know it?'

Writers, frail and imperfect like their fellow-mortals, are very apt to deceive themselves and their readers, in representing the motives which impel them both to compose and to publish their lucubrations.

If you think it worth while to inspect Prefaces and Dedications, you will find many authors declaring, that their chief motive to write is a desire to inform the understandings, or to correct the morals of the world, regardless of themselves, whether fame or obscurity is to be their final portion. They are contented to withdraw themselves so long as the public receive advantage. While the cause of truth is served, or science advanced, their end is fully answered.

If indeed *man* were a more perfect being than he is found to be in his most informed and improved state, we might believe that writers, who recommended liberality and public spirit with much strength of argument, were themselves possessed of those qualities in a degree which taught them to forget their own interest, as they sometimes profess, in their zeal to promote the welfare of the public; but few men are so elevated as to be divested of self-love. One writer may renounce money; but is impelled by fame: another may despise fame; but is actuated by the love of lucre. If a few have written merely to inform and amend their fellow-creatures, they must have been such as were remarkably elevated and enlightened by the pure principles of Christianity. Heathen philosophy and human learning produce not such moral heroism.

But what shall we say of those public-spirited writers who compose and publish with the liberal view of delivering us all from superstition, or of *disabusing* us of Christianity? They pretend to an uncommon share of benevolence, they are outrageously philanthropic, and, if their prefaces are to be believed, they mean only to liberate their fellow-creatures from the manacles of prejudice. But from the style of dictation which they assume, and the displeasure they express on being convicted of error and fallacy, there is reason to believe that they are under the influence of pride and selfishness; of that peculiar selfishness which leads them, for the sake of gratifying their vanity, and of obtaining distinction among those of whom they affect a contempt, to hazard the disturbance of the repose, and even the destruction of the human race.

There are doubtless many men who discharge the duties of life, in the civil and domestic circles, from a virtuous principle; and very often sacrifice both their ease and their pecuniary interest to the performance of them; but what man shall say, that it is his indispensable duty to write, and to print his writings, for the improvement of the public? Who gave him this commission? A man may have an inclination to write his thoughts, and he may also be impelled by the fine feelings of his genius; but will any man who *publishes*, declare that, in doing so, he has no other motive or stimulus whatever but the love of mankind? If he is a good man, he must wish that his productions may do good; and the hope that they will do good may have weight in prevailing on him to offer them to the public notice; but, I believe, there is commonly a mixture of vanity even in this laudable motive; and that, if he examines his heart, he will find in it a desire of distinction as a man of letters, and a love of literary fame. He wishes to raise himself while he serves others, and to buy distinction at the price of trouble*.

And allowing this to be so, where is the shame or culpability? Since there is no evil in being impelled to good and useful actions partly by the love of fame, why should authors studiously disavow that motive, and hypocritically declare, that they are impelled by no other principle than the desire of benefiting their fellow-creatures? Such pretensions are the mere cant of authorship; a flimsy covering, intended to conceal that which is no disgrace, since it is found to be the attendant of the most improved state of human nature.

I know of few better men, human errors excepted, or better writers than Cicero. But Cicero felt, and avowed, a love of fame; and has left it on record, as his opinion, that the best and noblest natures are the most powerfully actuated by the prospect of glory.

He who is sincerely influenced in publishing his sentiments by the love of God and man, without any commixture of pride and vanity, is, I must acknowledge, a much greater man than Cicero; and, if

---

* Digito monstrari et dicier hic est.—Hor.

To hear it said there, there he goes.

any thing can give him this elevation, I repeat, that
it must be 'the religion of Jesus Christ.' A man
who is deeply impressed with a sense of his duty
'as a Christian,' may be led to believe, and may, in
consequence of his belief, shew by his actions, that
all his *talents* are to be used in the immediate service
of him who gave them, in returning him praise, and
in diffusing happiness among his creatures to the
best of his abilities. But our gold has always a
great mixture of alloy; and he who ostentatiously
pretends, that the ore in his composition is perfectly
pure, is in danger of being considered as an impos-
tor. The very pretension to so much purity is itself
a particle of dross, and a proof of a base mixture.

Let not the author, on one hand, assume the appearance of unattainable excellence; and let not the
reader, on the other, expect or demand it. In the
present infirmity of human nature, it is sufficient
that good is intended and produced; though the
motive is not entirely free from vanity or self-interest.

I think it would be prudent, if authors would
cease to declare, that their publications are entirely
the effect of a regard for mankind, without any wish
for distinction or emolument. Such a profession, as
it is not rendered probable by uniform experience of
human nature in its most perfect state, conduces to
diminish the credit of an author, instead of advancing it, and therefore causes his book to have less
influence on those whom it was intended to benefit.
It savours of empiricism. The discerning part of
mankind always expect and make allowances for
some degree of self-love in every act of social beneficence.

Many, however, are inclined to expect from authors, that perfection which they see recommended
in their books, and are disgusted and disappointed
at beholding in them the common frailties and in-

firmities of human nature*. But if you expect the moralist to be uniformly as good as the morals he describes or recommends in his writings, then expect your physician to be always in health, or at least always able to cure his own disorders.

NUMBER XIII.

On the Absurd Affectation of Misery.—Ev. 13.

THE vanity of man may justly be termed a Proteus. In the endeavour to obtain distinction, not only happiness, but even misery is sometimes affected and even incurred.

I believe it is considered by many as honourable to possess a degree of that sensibility which is too delicate to bear the common asperities of human life ; and there is a style of complaint which is thought pretty, and a sort of woe which has been indulged not only as a luxury but as an occasion of pride. If I might borrow a term from criticism for the use of ethics, I would denominate the querulous affectation of misery, the elegiac style of life. The plaintive tone of elegiac language, and the soft tinge of melancholy, without any real cause, are very similar to the conversation and sentiments of those numerous complainers who have adopted the querulous style, because they considered it as extremely graceful.

* Quotusquisque philosophorum invenitur qui disciplinam non *ostentationem suæ scientiæ,* sed *legem vitæ* putet ?—CIC.

How few philosophers are there who do not rather make a parade of their learned systems, than suffer them to be the guides of their conduct?

I reverence the sorrows of the truly unhappy. Their tears are sacred. But those who affect a sensibility which they do not possess, and act a woe which they never felt, are to be considered as ridiculous and reprehensible, because they make a mock of human misery, and sport with that compassion which ought never to be abused, and which was designed for the comfort of unfeigned affliction.

I respect the character of Mr. Gray, as that of a man of remarkable virtue, learning, and genius, united. But he was melancholy without apparent reason; and, I apprehend, not entirely free from the wish to be considered as a man endowed with feelings unknown to the rest of his race. Every man of genius certainly has acute feelings; but those feelings will lead them to high enjoyments, and will make life more pleasurable than painful, if he will but submit to the guidance of his reason, and keep himself free from the affectation of singular misery. Pride, and an insatiable desire of praise, will indeed often cause, in the votaries of fame, pangs unknown to others, which cannot be reasonably indulged.

Many poets, professedly elegiac, have pretended to uncommon wretchedness; but they deceived no sensible reader, since it was evident that their misery was no less fictitious than their mythology.

The affectation of woe is chiefly among the softer sex, in whom it is sometimes supposed to have been amiable. Pity, it has been said, is nearly related to love. But the pity must be sincere. Affected woe will only excite affected pity, which is closely allied to a passion very different from love. Beauty in tears, while those tears are believed to be natural, must powerfully call for the protection of every man not destitute of generosity; but if the call is found to have been frequently made without sufficient reason, though it may cause the attention of false and selfish gallantry, it will not raise the sympathetic esteem of the estimable. She who wishes for such esteem, will be prudent in divesting herself of every kind of affectation.

I am sorry to see a taste prevail for novels which exhibit unnatural pictures of misery, and diffuse a love of the woeful. The novel entitled *Werter*, is of a bad tendency, and cannot have failed to have given the falsely delicate, the over-refined, and the idolizers of themselves, additional encouragement in the affectation of misery.

Mournful elegies, night thoughts, and contemplations on gloomy subjects, have a tendency to diffuse a shade over the imagination which causes in many a misery no less real than actual suffering; and they countenance more in seeking the gratification of a perverse vanity by pretending to singular wretchedness. There is certainly a great portion of evil in the world, real and unavoidable, and it seems a peculiar degree of folly to increase it by affectation. Affectation will increase it; for we become in time the characters which we have habitually assumed. In this country, where the inhabitants are naturally inclined to a dejection of spirits, it is particularly wrong to indulge the imagination in giving a sombrous and dismal colour to every thing around it. It is greatly in our power to make the horizon of our mind dark and cloudy, or serene as the blue ether, and beautiful as the variegated tints of a western sky in a fine summer evening.

It is a question in philosophy, *An quicquid recipitur, recipiatur ad modum recipientis,* '*Whether whatever is received* (or *perceived,* as it suits the present subject better) *be perceived according to the percipient's mode, or powers, or degree of perception?*' and I think it may be often answered, when applied to morals, in the affirmative. There is absolute good in life, and absolute evil; but they both may be in a great degree transformed by the manner in which they are viewed and possessed. A sour disposition, operating like a chemical acid, will turn the sweetest cup into an unpalatable beverage; as a contented, placid, meek, and gentle mind, infusing sweetness into the bitterest draught, will cause the most nauseous medicine to be swallowed with complacence.

To enjoy, and to be cheerful, are duties. 'To enjoy,' says Mr. Pope, 'is to obey.' And though it is natural, and often unavoidable, to complain in affliction; yet to murmur, repine, and take a pleasure in complaining, while we have many reasons to rejoice, is irrational and ungrateful.

The sect of whiners, or grumblers (for it deserves to be stigmatized by no very honourable name), furnishes a very proper subject for ridicule. It is fruitless to argue deeply or very seriously with folly and vanity. You will either not be understood by them, or not regarded; but a laugh against them, is like an instrument which touches to the quick, amputates the excrescence, or pulls it up by the roots.

Real misery will, I hope, always meet with sympathy. Nature has taken care that it should touch our feelings, in order to extort relief if possible. But the affectation of it, whether in books, in life, or in conversation, must find a different treatment, that it may be discountenanced.

Great caution, however, should be always used, not to mistake real for affected misery. It is better that many pretenders to woe should be treated with superfluous sympathy and unnecessary attention, than that one real sufferer should be disregarded.

NUMBER XIV.

On the Destruction of Ancient Mansion-houses.—Ev. 14.

It is not without concern, that men of taste and reflection behold the noble mansion-houses of our forefathers either utterly forsaken and fallen into ruins, or meanly sold under the hammer, for the price of the dismembered materials. Where the hospitable hearth once blazed, and the turret bell sounded cheerfully at noon, the owl now screams, the eft and the toad crawl unmolested, nettles and briars luxuriantly vegetate, and not one stone is left upon another to tell that here dwelt charity, heroism, and magnificence.

As I was wandering over the site of an ancient Baron's castle, the very rubbish of which had been sold to pay a debt of honour contracted at a chocolate house in St. James's-street, methought I saw one of its ancient inhabitants arising from the ground, and venting his feelings in the following soliloquy :—

'Accursed luxury, and false refinement! To you I must attribute the demolition of a pile which at once did honour to a race of worthies, and embellished the face of the country. It was built in a style of architecture characteristic of its inhabitants, bold, solid, substantial, and magnificent. Its gates opened to all the neighbouring gentry and yeomanry ; and the threshold was worn with the feet of the poor.

'Here stood the chapel. Though superstition sometimes deformed the altar, yet piety and charity made atonement for her errors. Hypocrisy and infidelity, affrighted at the lustre of their awful forms, never approached the place. It afforded solace to age, wisdom to the young, relief to the afflicted, and pleasure and improvement to all the illustrious family and to all the neighbours. But, alas! during fifty years previous to the stone-mason's purchase of the marble pavement, it was used as a dog-kennel; it was defiled with every abomination; and now the very site of it is overgrown with hemlock and deadly night-shade.

'Yonder was a room devoted to the purposes of a dispensary. The art of medicine was but indifferently understood; but what it could do, it did, with a bounty and benevolence that reflected honour on human nature. Ladies, high in rank and fashion, condescended to administer the salutary potion with their own hands, and to pour oil into the wounds of the traveller, and the poor destitute who had none to help him. Food, clothing, and instruction, completed the beneficence of the pious matron; who appeared with a dignity, in these humble offices, the loss of which, no titles, no finery, no studied graces, no fashionable airs of grandeur can compensate. I know it is common to say, that such bounty is no longer necessary, since the legal institutions of parochial relief have interposed. But what is the cold assistance, the compelled charity of an upstart and rigid officer, to the kind and voluntary relief afforded by the rich and great, actually and personally applying balm to the afflicted? What is the attendance of a hireling nurse, to the affection of a mother? The bounty and beneficence which is now censured and ridiculed, arose from Christian principles, and did more to promote them, than all the controversial divinity of all the divines united.

'On that ample area rose the spacious and lofty refectory. The first view of it struck the mind with ideas of grandeur and nobility which the modern saloon, with all its elegance, cannot emulate. The oaken tables were laden with plentiful food; with dishes

solid, natural, wholesome, unspoiled by the arts of fo-
reign cookery, which, to please a vitiated palate, converts the gifts of God designed for the sustenance of
man, to a slow but certain poison. A race of heroes
and heroines sat at the upper table; and the honest
rustic was cordially welcomed at the lower. The
species of fine gentlemen, powdered and essenced,
pale and languid, was unknown in those times, when
effeminacy had not reduced the manly form below
the standard of healthy women. I own there prevailed a bluntness of manners, which, in the present days,
would be deemed roughness; but it was a roughness
which led to generous acts in war, and taught a contempt of all mean and unmanly indulgence in peace.
I will not deny that the polish of the present time is
laudable; but it is often carried to excess: and let
it be remembered, that the file may be used till the
substance it was to adorn is rendered too thin and
weak to retain any value. Truth and sincerity, the
best embellishment of a man, are often lost in the
refinements of the highly-finished gentlemen of modern courts. But it is the province of art to improve
and adorn, not to extinguish nature.

'The hospitality which prevailed in that Gothic
hall is said to have encouraged gluttony and drunkenness. But, let it be considered that the food was
plain, though plentiful; the beverage homely, though
highly relished by the unspoiled palate. And let actual observation determine, whether gluttony, advanced to its highest degree by art; and drunkenness inflamed by exquisite wines and distillation, do not
disgrace the selfish orgies of the modern feast. In
the old times, the middle and the lowest orders were
permitted freely to partake the great man's banquet.
It contributed at once to their necessities and their
enjoyment. But at the table of modern luxury, the
superfluous viands are usually open only to those

who are already satiated with dainties, and know no appetite but that which high seasoning provokes. There remains all the intemperance, without the generosity, of our grandsires; all the vices of riot, without the virtues of charity to cover them.

‘ But allowing all that can be claimed by modern refinement, and I own that, in many things, it is to be preferred to the rudeness and grossness of less civilized times; yet I must bear my testimony against the prevailing practice of demolishing the noble edifices which the worthies of past times erected with a splendour equal to their munificence. I cannot bear to see the land desolated by mean avarice. I cannot bear to see the mansion of old bountiful families forsaken for the petty villa fit only for a retired trader. Taste, as well as manly virtue, suffer by such littleness when it appears in men, who are raised to distinction by the merits of those ancestors whom they despise.’ He was proceeding, when he was interrupted by the arrival of a smart young man, the lord of the land, with a pale face and meagre form, who sat lolling in his vis-à-vis with a hackneyed courtesan, drawn by four cropt grays, and driven rapidly over the site of the ancient castle. The venerable progenitor lifted up his hands and eyes with silent indignation, and then vanished in despair.

NUMBER XV.

On the desire of Distinction by living beyond an Income.—Ev. 15.

PHILOSOPHERS have often compared individuals of the human race to the various animals of the irrational creation. Some are said to resemble foxes, some hogs, and others asses; and the resemblance has been supposed to be so great as to contribute something to the support of the Pythagorean Metempsychosis. I believe the philosophers would not have erred, if, while they were reciting resemblances, they had said, that a great part of mankind are like the peacock, which appears to take its greatest pleasure, and to place its chief good, in the display of its finery. As to the transmigration of souls, some have thought that so great an attention to the gaudy appearance of the body, argues something in these persons against the existence of the soul at all; so that I do not pretend to corroborate, from the circumstance of their likeness to the bird of Juno, the whimsical doctrine of old Pythagoras.

To make a figure, to the utmost extent of their ability, is the ultimate scope of many; as to expand the plumage of its tail in all its pride is the supreme bliss of the peacock: whose internal qualities, and real value (which, by the way, are in that respect like those of the vain votaries of fashion), by no means correspond with the ostentatious appearance of the plumage.

As the desire of distinction is natural, so the wish to make a figure, even in externals, while it is limited by right reason, and urges not to the violation of prudence and justice, is innocent at least, though scarcely laudable. But it is found in this age to lead to an expensive mode of living, and to the affectation of a splendour greatly above what the rank of the parties require, and their fortunes can support.

The house must be larger, the servants more numerous, the table more luxurious, and the equipage more splendid, than either a sense of decorum, or a prudential regard to the permanent interest of the family, can admit. And what is the inducement? The hope of being received into company which assumes the envied title of people of fashion. The aspirants at this honour are indeed sometimes received; but if it is suspected that they make a show without much substance to support it, they are commonly held in low esteem; and the subterfuges they are obliged to use to conceal their inferiority, renders the state, which, after much difficulty, they have obtained, truly uneasy. They indeed enjoy, in fancy, the pleasure of gratified pride, and are too rapidly whirled in the circle which they have chosen, to find leisure for reflection. But this is a state which no rational creature, who possesses the faculty of which he boasts as his noblest distinction, can deem desirable. And yet, for the sake of this distinction, what sacrifices are made! Health, peace, and the plenty of a competency, are the usual price of the dear-bought purchase. Neither do these ostentatious people enjoy themselves sincerely; for they are conscious of imprudence and injustice; and however they may attempt to stifle the voice of reason, they will sometimes be compelled to hear it; if not at the assembly and masquerade, yet on their pillows, and in their chambers, when, after all their efforts to escape, they are under an unavoidable necessity of *communing with themselves, and of being still.*

The creditors and the children of the numerous tribes who live above their rank and fortune, experimentally feel and deplore that my representation is no fiction. Creditors wait so long for payment as to lose their profit in the interest, and often rejoice if they receive ten shillings in the place of twenty. Many of them have been reduced to beggary by supplying the vain with the necessaries of life; for it so happens, that those who supply superfluities, are often paid with ostentatious liberality and alacrity; while he who sells bread, meat, and raiment, is obliged to take out a commission of bankrupt, or sue in vain for his just due by a tedious and vexatious process of the law.

The children of *ambitious paupers** suffer cruelly. They are introduced into a walk of life which they must relinquish for ever on the departure of their parents. The money that should have been kept as a reservoir to supply their wants during life, in adversity, and in old age, has flowed in profusion to furnish superfluities in the season of health and youth. Their sentiments, habits, pleasures, and prospects, are all in high life; yet their fortunes are such as must detain them in a state of dependance, if not of servitude. But supposing enough left to enable a large family to live in competent plenty, yet, as they have been used to ostentation and luxury, that plenty which would otherwise have afforded comfort, and been considered as a blessing, is viewed in the light of penury and meanness; and that middle station, in which they were born, and might have enjoyed as much happiness as belongs to human nature, is deplored by them as a fallen state. Consequently, instead of feeling and displaying a cheerful and contented gratitude, they murmur and repine throughout their lives, at their unfortunate degradation.

I knew a family, the father of which had an old paternal estate of five hundred a year. There were five children to enjoy it with him while he lived, and to inherit it when he should die. But his lady was of opinion that he would serve his family most, by introducing them into company and life, and forming valuable connexions. The truth was, she loved a gay and dissipated scene, and was but too successful in persuading her husband to adopt her plan. A

---

* Hic vivimus ambitiosâ paupertate omnes.—Juv.

—————Though poor yet proud—we vie
With others in—ambitious poverty.

style and mode of living were immediately engaged
in, which would require, on the most moderate computation, one thousand a year. There was no mode
of increasing the income, the father having no profession, and being above trade. The whole time and
attention of the family was devoted to dress, fashionable diversions, and visiting a circle of neighbours,
some of whom were East India nabobs, baronets,
and lords. The consequence was unavoidable. On
the death of their parents, the children found that
every foot of land, and all the goods and chattels,
belonged to importunate creditors, who, after having
sustained a heavy loss, eagerly seized all the re-
mainder of property; so that they saw themselves,
literally, not worth a single shilling. They might,
with much reason, be unhappy in their situation, as
their hopes and prospects had once been so elevated;
but their misery was much increased by their inability to render themselves useful in society, and to
compensate the unkindness of their fortune by personal exertion; for they really had learned nothing
but the arts of dress, and the expensive modes of
fashionable life. Two of the sons were sent to the
East Indies by the interest of a compassionate neighbour: one took to the highway, and, after a narrow
escape, was obliged to transport himself into Africa:
the daughters went into service, but being above it,
were discarded with insults; till sick of attempting
in vain, one died of disappointment, and the other
sought dishonest bread in the misery of prostitution.
So ended the splendour, the luxury, the pride of a
family, which, if it could have been contented with
the comforts of a most valuable competency, might
at this time have been flourishing in reputation,
plenty, and prosperity. Many similar cases occur,
where the misery of innocent children has been
caused by the vanity of unthinking parents, led

astray by the *ignis fatuus* of vanity, aping the manners of high and fashionable life.

But what? is there no such thing as solid comfort with a moderate fortune, and in the middle state? Must we for ever labour to leave the rank in which Providence has placed us, in order to relish our existence? Must we be guilty of injustice and cruelty, in order to be happy? Believe it not. Things are not so constituted. But the votaries of vanity, though they may possess a good share of natural understanding, are usually furnished but slenderly with philosophy and religion. They know not how to choose for themselves the chief good; but, blindly following the multitude, suffer themselves to be led, in the journey of life, by the false light of a vapour, rather than by the certain guidance of the polar star, or the magnetic needle.

I wish I could induce them to consider duly the nature and value of *solid comfort*. But we do consider it, say they; we consider what pleases ourselves, and we pursue it with constancy. Are you convinced, I ask in return, that what you pursue affords you pleasure? Is it not true, on the contrary, that you live rather to please others than yourselves? You certainly live in the eyes of others; of others, as vain and proud of externals and of trifles as yourselves; and in their applause or admiration, you place your felicity. So long as you can display the tinsel appearance of gaiety and ease, you patiently submit to the real and total want of the substance. I urge you then again to pursue solid comforts, and relinquish vanity. You ask me to describe what I mean by solid comforts. It is easy to conceive them; but as you desire it, I will attempt the obvious enumeration, and then leave you to your own dispassionate and unprejudiced reflections.

Solid comforts may be copiously derived from the following sources: a quiet conscience, health, liberty, one's time one's own, or if not, usefully, innocently, and moderately, employed by others; a freedom from inordinate passions of all kinds; a habit of living within one's income, and of saving something for extraordinary occasions; an ability, arising from rational economy, to defray all necessary and expedient expenses; a habit of good humour, and aptitude to be pleased rather than offended; a preparation for adversity; love of one's family, sincerity to friends, benevolence to mankind, and piety to God.

Compare this state and these dispositions with those of affected people of fashion, embarrassed in circumstances, distressed by vain cares, tossed about by various passions and vain fancies, without any anchor to keep their frail bark from the violence of every gust. But it is not necessary to dilate on the comparison; let the hearts of the deluded votaries of vanity decide upon it in the silence of the night-season, when they recline on their pillows, when the lights of the assembly are extinguished, and the rattling of carriages is heard no more.

NUMBER XVI.

On the Retirement of Tradesmen and Persons long used to Business and Action, to Rural Life and the Employments of Agriculture.—Ev. 16.

THE pleasures of rural life form one of the common-places of the poets, and they have adorned it with the richest colours of fanciful description. He who believes their representations, will deem nothing more conducive to his happiness, than to fly to the remotest wilds, to forests dark with shade, to rivulets gliding over pebbles, to plains clothed with verdure, covered with flocks, and resounding with the shepherd's pipe. That pastoral poets should indulge in such luxuriant descriptions, is not wonderful: but even Horace, a man of the world and the poet of common sense, has, in some passages, yielded to the delusion, and endeavoured to extend it.

The *employments* of agriculture, and the life of the husbandman, have been also described by the poets, to use the language of Addison on another occasion, as

Profuse of bliss and pregnant with delight.

Under these two prepossessions, the one in favour of rural felicity, and the other of the joys of farming, the man of business in town, whether professional or commercial, has toiled for gain, with the hope of retiring into the country in middle or declining life; which he indulges with no less ardour, than if he were going into Elysium on the day of his long wished-for retreat from Cheapside.

But the blaze which imagination kindled has been extinguished on approaching it; the vision of happiness has vanished like a dream, on hastening to its actual enjoyment.

It is natural to inquire into the cause of the disappointment. Rural delights are certainly great; though exaggerated by the poets' fancy. Rural employments are certainly natural, amusing, and healthy; though extolled too highly, when represented as furnishing delight unalloyed with vexation.

Persons who retire to rural life raise their expectations too high, above the pitch which human enjoyments are ever found to attain. A golden age, when the earth brought forth her fruits with spon-

taneous exuberance, must be revived to satisfy the
ideas of felicity which they have connected with the
operations of agriculture.

Success in farming, and without success there can
be no pleasure in it, depends on the labours of those
who are commonly unwilling to labour hard for a
gentleman, or man of fortune, and who, under the
appearance of rustic simplicity, conceal a low cunning scarcely compatible with honesty. The defective work, the exorbitant demands, the discontented
dispositions of these persons, soon give a very different idea of rural swains, hinds, and shepherds,
than was received from the poets. These alone are
able to convince a man of his error who retires to a
farm as to an occupation of uninterrupted tranquillity.
Though his circumstances should be such as cannot
be affected by their injurious treatment, yet his
temper will probably be tried by their perverse behaviour. He may not be deeply wounded; but his
ease will be effectually destroyed for a time, though
he should only be scratched by a bramble, or pricked
by a thorn.

Inclement weather and unfavourable seasons, com-
bining with improper management, render the produce of the farm, after great expense and no little
solicitude, scanty and ill-conditioned. The object,
in a lucrative view, is perhaps inconsiderable; but
disappointment even in trifles, when the heart is set
upon them, is bitter. Thorns and briars, thistles
and nettles, are the crops where wheat was cultivated, or where figs and grapes were expected. Instead of seeing lands laughing with corn, the disappointed gentleman-farmer hangs, in a pensive pos-
ture, over the gate of the field, that smiles, as it were
in mockery, with the red poppy, the blue bugloss,
the yellow charlock, the white bearbind, the silky
mallow, and the feather-topped dandelion.

If he has purchased a little manor, the poacher plagues him with his wires, and the unqualified sportsman harasses him with trespasses. Every hare, partridge, and pheasant, that he sees dispatched to London, he believes to be stolen from himself. Neither night nor day can be spent in perfect security. His money he can lock up in his chest, but partridges have wings, hares are fleet, and poachers subtle and indefatigable. The carp and tench are stolen from his ponds. School-boys and idle neighbours insnare his trout, and troll for his pike, without his permission. All these things render, what amuses and profits others, a mortification to the poor possessor*.

If he delights in a garden, there also vexation will spring up among the choicest fruits and flowers. See yonder wall most beautifully covered with peaches, that blush like the cheeks of Hebe or Maria. He has chosen the trees with the nicest judgment, trained them with incessant care, and now they are ripe; and to-morrow the finest shall be culled, for it is Maria's birthday. To-morrow's sun arises, and, lo! the wall is stripped. Some caitiff, at the midnight hour, plucked them all with unrelenting hand, and by this time they are safely lodged in Covent-garden market.

He delighted in poultry. He fed the chickens and ducklings with his own hand. He chose the most beautiful in plumage, the largest in size, the finest for the table. But the soldiers quartered in the neighbourhood, and that varlet, Reynard, have stolen them all, but a few that were shut up in a coop to be fattened for new-year's day. These, however, he preserves; but upon computing the ex-

* Et dominum fallunt et prosunt furibus.—Hor.

The owner loses and the thief obtains.

pense, he finds that he might have bought them much fatter and finer of farmer Hodge at half the expense.

He fattens his own hogs, and every bit of pork stands him in double the money he could buy it for at the butcher's. He keeps a dairy, but the cows die with disease, the calves are still-born, the butter rancid for want of care, and the milk sour. Hodge would supply his table with every article, cent. per cent. cheaper than he can make it at home, without trouble, or the hazard of a bad commodity.

Fortunately for the crows and the dogs, he keeps a little flock of sheep, with the prettiest musical bells ever heard in the country. But for want of skill and care in the management, half of them die of the rot, or are worried by the mastiff to death. Those which he kills, furnish his table with an inferior mutton as dear as venison.

He brews his own beer, presses his own cider, and bakes his own bread; but three times out of four the beer has an ill taste, through want of skill and cleanliness of the casks; the cider is vapid; and the bread, luckily for the pigs, heavy.

Add to this and a thousand other mortifications of a similar kind, that the comforts of neighbourhood are often destroyed by causes which appear trivial, but are very momentous in a village. The squire rides over his seed in hunting, breaks down his painted Chinese pales, and saws off the first rail of his seven-barred gate, which he had caused to be made, with great taste, by a London carpenter. The clergyman demands tithes of his sheep, pigs, poultry, eggs, and milk; and as he is determined to resist extortion, he goes to law for five shillings, and is cast with costs that amount to a hundred pounds. No neighbourly intercourse can continue. So far from a comfortable reciprocation of good offices, that scarcely common civility is observed. Not even a bow at church, or the common salutation of a ' how do you do ?' when the parties meet by the casualties of the day. Rural sociality is often bound by cobweb bands.

Thus uncomfortable, he is ready to exclaim with sighs,

> Vitæ me redde priori.—Hor.
>
> O ! make me what I was before.

and looks back with regret on the ease, plenty, liberty, and society of the city which he once detested.

But I do not mean that a conclusion should be drawn, that the country and rural employments are not able to furnish much pleasure. My wish is, to convince persons who retire into the country late in life, for ease only*, that they must not raise their expectations of rural happiness too high ; and that in pursuit of ease, they ought not to engage in farming to any great extent, because it is an employment full of anxiety and care, subject to much disappointment, and as little adapted to procure ease, as the commerce of the busy trader, the employments of the statesman, the lawyer, or the physician. He who wishes, on retirement, to enjoy all the tranquillity which the country can afford, should rather be a spectator than a sharer in the employments of agriculture ; and be satisfied with inhaling the sweet air, and viewing the delightful scenes of the country, without troubling himself, unless he is skilled in husbandry, to raise and produce those necessary commodities of life, which he may purchase at the market cheaper and better without any anxiety.

* ──── ut in otia tuta recedant.—Hor.

To find a safe recess.

NUMBER XVII.

*On Xenophon's Memoirs of Socrates, and the Inferiority of Translations to the Originals.—*Ev. 17.

A PERSON who should walk about the streets of a great city like Athens or London, and give his opinion on all subjects to those whom he might happen to meet, would be thought, in the present age, a ridiculous enthusiast, or a pitiable madman. Yet it is certain, that he whom the world has long revered as the wisest of mortals, dispensed his advice in this manner, and was, while alive, the object of envy rather than of contempt, as he has been since his death, of admiration.

Socrates committed not the philosophy which he thus disseminated to writing: and the world would have been deprived of the inestimable treasure, if his grateful scholars, Xenophon and Plato, had not preserved it.

Xenophon's *Memorabilia*, or Memoirs of him, abound with a most admirable morality; yet I hope the admirers of ancient wisdom will pardon me, when I presume to say, that many of the conversations are tediously protracted, and that the great Socrates, in the abundance of his good-humour, trifles egregiously. It is, however, equitable to suppose, that, to insinuate his important advice with success, it was necessary to avoid alarming the minds of his hearers, and that the beginning of his conversations should have an air of alluring levity. This levity was probably in unison with the minds of those careless passengers whom he addressed. It drew their attention. They would have shut their ears against every thing which he had to offer, if he had begun by professing a design to reclaim them from vice and folly, in a formal and severe harangue. They would have hastened from him, and turned his attempts to ridicule. But his jocularity detained them, and his good sense, in the conclusion, pointed out their errors, and taught them the expediency of a reformation. Yet though this may apologize for levity and trifling, in the actual conversations of the living Socrates, it cannot render them entirely agreeable to a judicious reader of modern times, for whom the artifice is not necessary.

I read Xenophon's Memorabilia in Greek, while at school, and I was delighted with them. I read them afterward in an English translation, and I found them in many places tedious and insipid. The translation was apparently performed with sufficient fidelity; but it did not affect or strike with any peculiar force. I have experienced effects exactly similar to this in the perusal of other books in the most celebrated translations. To what shall I attribute them? Are there such charms in the Greek language, as are able to give a value to sentiments which of themselves have no recommendation? Certainly not: but there is a conciseness, and, at the same time, a force and comprehension of expression in the Greek language besides its harmony, which, I think, the English cannot equal. On the mind of a reader, who completely understands the language of a Greek author, the ideas are impressed with more vivacity and perspicuity by the original, than by any translation into modern languages. The ancient Greek authors, it is acknowledged, paid great attention to the art of composition, to the choice and arrangement of words, and to the structure of periods; so as to communicate the idea, or raise the sentiment intended, with peculiar force and precision.

Xenophon is known to have been one of the most successful cultivators of the art of composition; and it cannot be supposed, that all who have undertaken to translate his works, though they might understand the matter, could have equalled him in style and expression, for which his country and himself were remarkably celebrated. To represent him adequately they must have possessed a style in English equal to his style in Greek.

The pleasure which a reader feels in the perusal of a Greek author, has been attributed to the pride of conscious superiority, over those who are not able to unlock the treasures of which he keeps a key. This opinion has owed its origin to the poor appearance which some of the most celebrated authors of antiquity have made, when presented to the public in the dress of a modern language. The English reader has read translations of the classics, without being able to discover any excellence adequate to the universal reputation of the authors. The translator, though he comprehended his author, and was faithful as to the *meaning*, was perhaps a *poor writer*, unable to communicate properly the thoughts which he conceived with a sufficient degree of accuracy. The blame unjustly fell on the original author, and on his admirers. *He* was supposed to have written poorly, and *they* to have admired him only from motives of pride and pedantical affectation. Some, whose ignorance prevented them from deciding fairly, rejoiced to see that ancient learning, which they possessed not, despised; and eagerly joined in attributing to arrogance and pedantry all praise of Greek and Latin, to which they were inveterate enemies, as well as perfect strangers. Thus Greek and Latin studies fell into disrepute.

But the supposition that the pleasure which men feel in reading authors in the ancient languages,

arises solely, or chiefly, from the pride of possessing
a skill in those languages, is too unreasonable to be
generally admitted. Of the many thousand admirers
of the ancients, who, in every part of their conduct
and studies, displayed great judgment and love of
truth, must we suppose the greater part, either deceived in the estimate of the authors whom they
read, or actuated by pride, and mistaking the self-
complacency of conscious learning and ability, for
the pleasure naturally arising from the study of a
fine author? Why is not a man, who understands
Welsh, German, Dutch, or any other language not
remarkable for literary productions, as much inclined
to extol the writers in those languages, as the reader
of Greek and Latin, if the motive for praise consists
only in possessing a knowledge of a language unknown to the majority of his countrymen or companions?

In accounting for the great esteem in which the
Greek and Latin authors are held, much must be attributed to the *languages solely*, exclusively of thought,
doctrine, or method. Many of our English readers,
who are but poorly qualified to give an opinion on
the subject, will impute it to pedantry, when I say,
that those languages possess inherent beauties, and
an aptitude for elegant and expressive composition,
to which the best, among modern languages, can
make no just pretension. Till, therefore, an ancient
Greek author can be translated into a language equal
to his own, it will be unjust and unreasonable to
form a final judgment of him from the best translation. It is better to read a good author in a translation, than not to read him at all. I only contend
against the injustice of condemning original authors
in consequence of the unavoidable imperfections of
all translations into the modern languages of Europe.

But, to return to Xenophon's Memorabilia, with

the consideration of which I began this paper. It has been usual, among the admirers of Socratic morality, to compare it with the evangelical. I am ready to acknowledge the great excellence of it; but I see clearly, that it is no more to be compared to the gospel, than the river Nile to the Pacific Ocean. It seems not to flow from the heart, and it cannot reach its recesses. It knows little of universal charity. It taught not the golden rule of doing to others as we wish they should do unto us.

I cannot, however, avoid recommending the Socraticæ Chartæ, or the fine Ethics of Socrates, as preserved by Xenophon and Plato, to every student who is designed for the sacred profession. He will there find a store of fine observations, maxims, and precepts, which he may recommend with authority and success to his people, under the sanction, and with the improvements, of Christianity*.

Dr. Edwards's attempt to discover *a system* in the Memorabilia of Socrates, notwithstanding its ingenuity, seems to be unsuccessful. It resembles the ingenious efforts of the critics to reduce Horace's Epistle ad Pisones on the Art of poetry, to the methodical regularity of a technical recipe for making poems. Some critics, like the old gardeners, have no idea of beauty, unless every thing is laid out by the line and rule, the level and the square. But mathematical precision is not required in moral disquisition.

---

* Socraticæ Chartæ   quem non fecère disertum?—Hor.
Socratic lore with   eloquence inspires.

NUMBER XVIII.

On a Species of Injustice in Private Life.
In a Letter.—Ev. 18.

' SIR,

'THERE is a species of injustice and cruelty in parents to their children, which has not, I think, been stigmatized with the infamy which it justly deserves. It is not uncommon in fathers, to permit the visits of a lover to his daughter, till the affections of both are engaged, and a clandestine marriage takes place; and then to profess a great dislike to the match, and a very warm displeasure, merely to avoid the payment of a portion. If the father is asked, why he encouraged the lover at first; he answers, that he did not imagine that he visited as a lover, though it was evident enough to every one else, and could not, from the attention paid, be unobserved by the father. The truth is, that he saw with pleasure the mutual passion, and gave every opportunity for its increase, by furnishing opportunities of intercourse, by studied occasions of absence; and even knew of the intended marriage, and took care to be from home at the time he expected it to be celebrated, lest by some accident he should be obliged to make the full discovery, which would frustrate his purpose. This disingenuous and crafty conduct is often productive of great misery.

' Mr. Marston was a young surgeon of good connexions, good abilities, good person, and with a competent income, from a place under government. Having a prospect of settling very advantageously in a genteel neighbourhood, he thought it proper to seek a matrimonial alliance. He visited in the fa-

mily of a physician of no great practice, who had
several very accomplished and beautiful daughters,
the eldest of whom, Eliza, soon attracted his particular attention. He made no secret of his attach-
ment, but openly avowed it, and behaved with all
the frankness of an honourable lover. He could
not but consider the father's silence as a tacit consent: but, after the expiration of two years assiduous
and successful courtship, he asked the permission
of the father to fix a day for the celebration of the
nuptials. The father, at the mention of it, started
back with affected astonishment, and peremptorily
insisted on his discontinuing to visit at his house.
No entreaties could avail, and Mr. Marston retired
in disconsolate acquiescence. But the links of love
were not to be broken. The father went a journey
into the North, and the lovers seized the opportunity of cementing a union by marriage, which they
did not doubt would soon be sanctioned by the approbation of a parent, who could not but have observed the commencement and increase of their
mutual affection.

' The father returned. The young couple wanted
only his approbation to complete their felicity.
They waited upon him together, and in terms of
affectionate duty, solicited his pardon and his blessing. He received them with a haughtiness and
severity which he had never before displayed; and
told them, on their departure, never more to approach his house, for he should give orders to his
servants to deny him, whenever they should come
to his door.

' After the lapse of some time, when they expected his severity might be mitigated by reflection, they
applied to him by a letter, expressing their hope,
that as he had not discouraged Mr. Marston's first
visits, but suffered a passion to grow under his eye,

he would not be implacably angry with them, for conduct which was the natural consequence of such indulgence. A respectful hint was added, that as he signified his intention to give his daughter a small fortune on their marriage, it would now be particularly acceptable, as Mr. Marston wanted to take a genteel house and furnish it, without which measure it would be difficult, if not impossible, to enter on the practice of his profession with a prospect of success.

'No answer was given to this letter during several months; when, on a second remonstrance, a verbal message was sent by the father, informing them, that as they had followed their own inclinations without consulting him, they must take the consequences, and live upon love if they could, for that he should not give them a single penny before his decease. It was added, that they need not apply any more; for this resolution was not the effect of a momentary fit of displeasure, but the result of the maturest deliberation.

'Mr. Marston, rather than involve himself in debt, retired to lodgings in a little village, hoping that time would effect a reconciliation, and produce that pecuniary assistance, without which he found it impossible to be established. Year after year elapsed, with an increase of family, and a consequent increase of expenses. He endeavoured to obtain a little country practice, but though he was much respected, the profits of a surgeon only, unconnected with the business of an apothecary, added but little to his income, and he was obliged to incur debt, which, notwithstanding the utmost frugality, amounted in time to a considerable sum. No assistance came from the father, who loving money above all things, continued to accumulate his store with the most miserly parsimony. But as the father was old, Mr. Marston thought he could not long be kept from that portion which he thought himself entitled to, and which was indeed now become necessary to his family's subsistence. Many years had passed in this uncomfortable situation, when grief and anxiety, which had long preyed on Mr. Marston's bosom, put a period to his existence at the age of thirty-six, and left a widow and eight children, with scarcely enough to procure the necessaries of the day. The old gentleman now relented; but it was too late. He, who by his abilities in his profession, might have raised his family to opulence, was gone for ever; and his companion, agitated by every feeling which wears away a tender frame, soon followed him. Eight orphans stood round the grave in which the tenderest of parents were both deposited. Every spectator was affected with sympathy except the father, who, while the clergyman performed the office, was railing at the undertaker in the churchyard, for supplying a handsomer and more expensive coffin than he had ordered.

' The children, whom he would not speak to, were sent to the house of a poor mechanic, with orders to clothe them cheaply, and take care of them, till they were respectively of age to be put out apprentices. Destitute of education, and without a true friend to guide them, they turned out unfortunately, ran away from their trades, entered in low situations into the army and navy, married imprudently, or died early of intemperance. Thus a family became wretched and extinct, which, if it had been fostered, as it ought to have been, by the parent who encouraged the first advances of a lover, from the mean idea of getting rid of the expense of a daughter, would have probably lived in a respectable and happy condition.

Wretched avarice! despicable cunning! which can

thus dissolve the closest bands of nature, and produce misery of the deepest kind, among those whom a parent is bound by all that can bind the human bosom, to render as easy and happy as the condition of humanity will allow.

'Let the trick of a father who encourages or connives at the visits of a lover till mutual affection is rivetted, and after the consequent marriage affects anger as an excuse for saving his money, be henceforth considered as infamous; and let young men, who have a just value for their own happiness, and the happiness of the women whom they love, be henceforth on their guard, lest they fall into a snare so contemptible and mischievous.'

NUMBER XIX.

On the Rashness of young and adventurous Writers in Medicine.—Ev. 19.

WHENEVER men of liberal education and long experience have presented their medical remarks to the public, they have justly obtained the praise of ingenuity and benevolence. Fame increased their practice, and practice rewarded them with well-earned opulence. Who can deserve it better, than he, of whom it can justly be said, that he is* OPIFER PER URBEM, in his practice, and PER ORBEM, in his communications to the public?

But others, observing that such have owed their cele-

---

* *Opifer per Orbem* is the motto of the Apothecary's company. It is said of Apollo, in Ovid's Metamorphoses. Applied to the medical assistant it signifies, 'one ready to afford universal medical assistance.'

brity, and consequently their fortunes, to a pamphlet or treatise, on some particular disease, have resolved, at all events, to write and publish a pamphlet or treatise, as soon as they have bought their diploma, or as an introduction to that honour.

In order to attract notice, it became necessary to *distinguish* their works, among a multitude of others, by some extraordinary doctrine or position; and I am informed, that things of a most dangerous tendency, and sometimes certainly fatal, have been plausibly recommended by fool-hardy or knavish candidates for medical popularity. AUDE ALIQUID*, *strike a bold stroke*, seems to be considered by many as a prescription for procuring practice.

The great object of such persons is to recommend something *new*, something extraordinary, something that marks a genius, either as a medicament, or as a chirurgical operation. If poison can be administered, in any form, without certain and immediate death, it is soon advanced to the rank of a *panacea*, and the inventor hopes to equal Radcliffe in riches, and Heberden in fame.

Time shews the inefficacy of the boasted invention; but it is to be feared, that many fall victims to it, before the full discovery of its ill effects, or the danger of relying upon it because of its inutility, in extreme or difficult cases.

Whoever takes a retrospective view of medicines which a few years ago were highly extolled, and generally used, will find many of them at present in total disrepute. Yet, if you will believe the writings, which recommended them on their first appearance, their beneficial efficacy was indubitably confirmed by innumerable cases. If they were efficacious once,

* Aude aliquid brevibus gyaris vel carcere dignum.—Juv.

Dare something worthy of the hulks or jail
Or Botany's famed bay.

they are probably still efficacious; for it is not to be believed that, by any causes whatever, the human body can have undergone a total change since their introduction. But they are now perhaps pronounced by the best judges utterly inefficacious or pernicious; and there is reason therefore to conclude that they were always so; and owed their popularity and success to novelty, or to the activity, address, and recommendation, of some artful professor of medicine.

But though the world might profit by uniform experience of the fallacy of medical pretensions, yet, as there is always a new generation rising, the same arts are again practised, and practised with dangerous success. In nothing are men more easily deluded than in the pretensions of medical practitioners.

It must be acknowledged, that the temerity of making experiments may casually lead to improvements in medical science; but it is a cruel temerity; for experiments in medicine are made on the sick at the hazard of life. A young man who hastily recommends to the public a powerful medicine, without due experience of its effect, which is too common in the present times, may be guilty of homicide, in a thousand melancholy instances, when he intended only to advance his own fame and fortune.

The spirit of research and adventure is indeed laudable in young men; but, when it produces works to the public which endanger health and life, it ought to be under greater restraint, than the sanguine disposition of raw practitioners, inventors, and projectors, is willing to allow. I appeal however to their humanity; and hope they will condescend to submit their treatises, previously to publication, to three or four of the most eminent and oldest physicians (or surgeons, if the subject be chirurgical), and even after that, to express themselves with doubt and diffidence on the certainty of their discoveries and the infallibility of their remedies. They will act humanely as well as prudently, by adding a Chapter of Cautions in the use of whatever they recommend.

Indeed, if medical publications were read only by medical professors and practitioners, there is reason to hope, that the rashness of a writer might be corrected by the caution and skilful experience of the *professional* reader. But, in these times, every man and woman reads a book, in which they think themselves interested; and the *sanguine* pamphlet of a young physician, who is able to dress his fancies in a language tolerably agreeable and perspicuous, falls into the hands of those, who are totally ignorant of medicine, both practical and theoretic, and who, imagining their own case to be exactly described in the book, take the medicine, just as it is prescribed, without regard to the difference of age, seasons, or symptoms. Constitutions are thus ruined by those who speciously pretend to have discovered their preservative.

It is a sad instance of human depravity, that, from motives of sordid interest or foolish vanity, men will trifle and tamper with the health and lives of their fellow-creatures, especially when their profession is to cherish health and prolong life.

But since there is no reason to suppose that rash physicians will discontinue the practice of publishing their crudities, it is certainly right to advise invalids, and all inexperienced persons who are not in the medical and chirurgical profession, not to read any books whatever on the subject of physic. This advice is indeed proper, even when the books are acknowledged to be solid, and known to be authenticated by the long practice of the writers; for, such is our weakness, especially in the hour of sickness, that we are apt to imagine every bad symptom, and almost every disease of which we read, to be our own : and the power of the imagination in augmenting disease, is not only well known to physicians, but felt by general experience.

After all that can be said in praise of medicine, it is confessed, by the most sensible physicians, to be a very doubtful point, whether, upon the whole, it has been more beneficial or injurious. It is an uncertain art. This point, however, is not uncertain, but very clear, that in the hands of the young, the inexperienced, and the rash, it is dreadfully destructive of the human race. What must it be, then, when *every man is his own physician?* When he reads a crude pamphlet on a disease under which he supposes himself to labour, and, without any preparatory knowledge, administers boldly whatever is recommended in the confidence of ignorance, or with the specious persuasion of a self-interested writer? Abstain, therefore, from medical books ; and apply, in sickness, to the best physician or apothecary within reach of your situation. Professional men themselves do not usually prescribe for themselves or families, in extreme cases ; but call in the assistance of those, who, with every advantage of speculative and practical skill, have also the additional advantage of being able to act with a cooler and more deliberate judgment than any man can usually exert, when his own health and happiness are deeply interested.

Among the inconveniences attending the multitude of books in the present times, it is one, that every man is instructed by some interested divulger of mysteries, to be his own operator or counsellor in every department. Every man may be his own Lawyer, Physician, Divine, Gardener, Broker, and Builder. This, it might be supposed, would injure the several professors ; but experience seems to prove that it serves them; every man attempting every thing for himself, without experience, and solely by the partial and imperfect directions of books, renders every thing he undertakes worse; and the professor is called in at last, and finds much more employment, than if his assistance had been sought before the bungling efforts of ignorance had rashly interposed.

NUMBER XX.

On the Books and Fugitive Writings which are proper for the Amusement of small portions of Leisure.— Ev. 20.

THERE are fragments of time in the life of every man, which, from some inconvenience of his circumstances, he is unable either to read with continued attention, or to enjoy the advantages of select company. In those intervals, such books are pleasant as amuse and inform, in very short sections or chapters, and in an easy and perspicuous style, resembling, as much as possible, the variety and familiarity of conversation.

Many of the French books, under the title of ANA, are, I think, particularly useful for the purpose of filling up a vacant interval. They are lively and various. They treat of history, literature, arts; subjects which amuse, without interesting in such a degree, as to fatigue or excite the mind beyond the pitch of a pleasant and equable tranquillity.

There is a great difference in the numerous *ana.* The best I ever read are not entitled *ana* indeed; but they are exactly the same in their kind; I mean

Melanges d'Histoire et de Literature, par Monsieur Vignoul Marville. The name of the real author, it is said, was D'Argonne. The work abounds with pleasing anecdotes, written with grace and vivacity. The part I am displeased with is, the severe hypercriticism on Bruyere. It is ingenious, but uncandid, and could proceed only from pique and prejudice. But I am speaking of amusement; and even mistaken criticism, written in the lively manner of D'Argonne, cannot but form an agreeable diversion in an interval of calm leisure.

Gesner recommends *ana* for the *horæ subsecivæ,* and also Choffin's *Amusemens Philologiques,* Martial's Select Epigrams, Owen's Epigrams, Epictetus, Bouhours's *Pensees Ingenieuses,* Phædrus, De la Motte, Fontaine, Valerius Maximus, Erasmus's Apophthegms, and all other similar and detached pieces. None of these require great attention or exertion, and yet they amuse and instruct in a very agreeable manner.

Selden's ' *Table Talk,*' would be called according to the French fashion, *Seldeniana,* and it is very proper for a pocket companion. Maxims and reflections, collections of poetry, letters, and fugitive pieces, with which this country abounds, are well adapted to the purpose of occasional amusement.

Indeed, the kind of books is sufficiently obvious: and it is not necessary to enumerate them. They must occur spontaneously to every man acquainted with books; but, in the present times, they are all in danger of being entirely superseded by the newspapers.

The newspapers, as they are now improved, are indeed *Melanges* of literature, of history, of criticism, of biography, of politics, of philosophy, of religion, and of every thing that busy mortals pursue with ardour and solicitude.

Their original object was the communication of political news; but they have increased in number, and in size, to such a degree, that, to fill them all with a due variety of news, properly so called, is impossible. That source was soon dry, and other fountains were therefore broken up. There can indeed be no good objection to the deviation from the original purpose of political news; for the intention of that was to amuse by the gratification of curiosity; and, if innocent amusement of a similar kind can be obtained in the heterogeneous matter which they exhibit, they are still valuable and worthy of encouragement.

But in pursuit of distinction and variety, in the gratification of party resentment, and as the tools of faction, many of them have displayed a foul mass of falsehood, malignity, and folly; such *personal* calumny and detraction, as degrades human nature, and could only have been expected from the agency of infernal spirits supplying the press of a Pandæmonium.

It is therefore become desirable to turn the eye from the public waste in which nettles and weeds, at once poisonous and putrid, vegetate, to cultivated gardens and enclosures. Such are most of the French *ana*, the *Melanges* and miscellanies of literature, history, and morality, which I recommend, as the proper amusement of a vacant hour.

The undertaking may be thought to resemble the cleansing of an Augean stable, and to require an Herculean strength, else one might endeavour to produce that desirable object, a reformation of venal and corrupt newspapers. The channels which convey polluted waters might be taught to devolve a pleasant and salubrious stream.

The conductors of newspapers, as many of them are most respectable men, would probably rejoice to see such a reformation, as might enable them to pursue their useful occupations, and promote their private interest, without the necessity of being instrumental to the diffusion of poison through the various ranks of society.

Suppose then that, by mutual agreement, they should oblige themselves to admit nothing which could degrade ' well-earned dignity, or injure reputation, or interrupt the peace of families,' without ascertaining the truth of it, by requiring its authenticity to be confirmed by the name of all parties, who should desire to insert a defamatory letter or paragraph.

This precaution would exclude some truth; but it would, at the same time, exclude more falsehood and misrepresentation; and newspapers would rise in value and repute, as they would be considered as authentic and respectable records worthy of being consigned to posterity.

If the papers were not of so large dimensions as they are, there would not be a necessity of supplying a quantity of matter merely to fill the columns; and, consequently, a more scrupulous selection might take place.

The king for the time being, and the judges his representatives, the church, and all its ministers, as well as all religious instructors, of whatever denomination, should always be mentioned in respectful terms. Their titles and honourable additions should be joined to their names, wherever it can be done without affectation, or tedious formality. It should be considered, that newspapers go into the hands of the vulgar, the ignorant, the idle, the profligate, the thievish, and the abandoned, of every degree and species; and that when once these are taught to speak disrespectfully of their superiors, whether ecclesiastical or civil, much of that subordination is disturbed, which was settled for the benefit of all; and much of that restraint infringed, which tended to keep them within due limits for the general advantage. Lawless principles naturally produce lawless actions: and there is every reason to believe, that much of the dishonesty of the lower orders, much of the riotous spirit of modern times, has been caused by the corruption of newspapers. I speak my thoughts freely, though I know the editors of newspapers have vengeance in their own hands, and are able to repel their assailants, with a lash of scorpions. But the shield of truth is a sufficient defence, and indeed a wound, in a good cause, makes an honourable scar.

Affairs of gallantry, as they are called, should be mentioned, if mentioned at all, with great delicacy. The mention of them at all, unless in cases of particular notoriety, tends only to confirm the impudence of parties concerned, and to increase debauchery by the seduction of example. It was lately usual to fill half a column in certain papers, with paragraphs, to puff the fashionable courtesans of the time, and to serve their interest. It is wonderful that papers, abounding in these subjects, can find admission into regular families, where there are wives and daughters of unsullied reputation.

There are some advertisements so evidently fraudulent, and others so grossly indecent, that he who aspires at the character of a good citizen, will find it difficult to render the publication of them consistent with such a description.

It is not difficult to point out the deformities of some among the public papers; for the features are prominent; but it is unnecessary. All considerate persons must have considered some prints, particularly where important truth is suppressed by influence, and defamation paid for with public money, as

pests and nuisances. I quit the subject, assuring
the reader, that I have no personal cause of dislike
to any of them. I disapprove of those which to
serve a party, sacrifice truth, justice, and mercy, because I think them publicly injurious. They have
been inimical to all order, propriety, moderation; to
virtue, to learning, and to religion: therefore an
endeavour to reform them can want no apology. I
will add only one hint to the conductors of them
which may avail when others are ineffectual. Let
them consider, that by degrading newspapers from
that dignity which they might possess, as pleasant
and useful vehicles of authentic information, and as
the most effectual defences against violence and
despotism, they may gradually render them too contemptible for general notice. The wickedness of
mankind, and the corruption of society may make
such an event not very probable at present; yet it
is certain that, in process of time, newspapers may
become so worthless, so utterly destitute of truth, as
to be universally neglected.

If manners do not effect the reformation of newspapers, laws may hereafter intervene to supply the
defect: and since it is the part of the legislature,
and of all good government, to suppress every general nuisance, it may be apprehended that the press
may be unfortunately restrained, and newspapers
abolished or discouraged by an enormous impost.
Nothing but the revenue arising from them preserves
them at present from some limitations, and which
would render them beneficial to society, without that
commixture of evil which almost overbalances their
advantages.

With all their imperfections on their heads, they
are upon the whole the best bulwarks of our liberty,
and the surest defence of the helpless against the
proud man's contumely and the oppressor's wrong.

They sound the alarm-bell throughout an empire,
and no influence is great enough to stifle the sound
before the people examine into its cause. Let u
bear all their evils, rather than endanger the libert
of the press.

NUMBER XXI.

On imitating a Model for the conduct of Life.—Ev. 21

MANY of the rules of rhetoricians contribute little to
the improvement of the orator, and serve only to
display the professor's subtilty. But the advice,
which they give on *the subject of imitation,* is truly
valuable, as it conduces immediately to facilitate
practice. They instruct their scholars, after the
preparatory learning is acquired, to choose a model
of style, according to which they may shape their
own; and not only the best writers and orators, but
also the best painters, sculptors, and architects, have
found that the easiest and most infallible mode of
acquiring, what the Greeks call ἕξιν, an *habitual ease*
in the practice of their arts, is to *follow the footsteps*
of some excellent predecessor.

The art of life may derive advantage from rules
intended only to facilitate the acquisition or practice
of *those humbler arts,* which administer to pleasure,
to pride, or to convenience. Let him who wishes to
live well, like him who wishes to write well, *choose a
model;* which he may imitate with a judicious and
discriminating, and not with a blind and servile, imitation.

A caution is necessary, lest the imitation recommended should become an odious species of affected

resemblance, lest it should be so close as to destroy all originality, and lest it should degenerate to an apish mimicry*. Such an imitation must be contemptible. Seneca gives a good idea of the sort of resemblance to be sought, when he says, ' the imitator of a style should endeavour to be like the original, not with the same exactness as a picture is like the person represented, but as a child resembles the features of its parent.' *Similem esse te volo, quomodo, filium, non quomodo imaginem.* I would have you *like*, as a son; not as a statue.

The first care is to select a proper person for a pattern, and then to discriminate between the qualities in his character which are suited to our genius, situation, rank in life, and profession, and those which, however admirable in him, would be ill-placed and ridiculous in us. Without this attention, we shall fall into the error of those whom an illustrious pattern leads into an imitation of its faults together with its beauties; we shall be affected, and lose our native character, without gaining in its place an adscititious one of equal value.

A judicious man will naturally select some person for imitation in the same profession or employment, of similar views, and of eminence in the particular walk of life, into which himself has entered. Common sense directs to such a choice. A clergyman, for instance, will imitate a clergyman; a lawyer, a lawyer; a physician, a physician; and so in all other departments of life.

The character, which forms the model, may be either living or dead. There are many lives of men in all professions written with accuracy, and with a minute detail of particular circumstances. Such

---

* Simia quàm similis, turpissima bestia, nobis!—ENNIUS.

How like the ape, that filthiest beast, to man!

models as these may be often better known, and
more easily imitated, than living characters, especially by young men, who cannot be much acquainted with the world, at least with eminent persons, in a degree sufficient to know all the requisite
circumstances concerning them.

I will descend to particulars. Suppose the young
man in orders, and that he fixes upon some eminent
character, by which to regulate his private life and
his parochial conduct. Suppose that person to be
Bishop Wilson, or Dr. Hammond, or Dr. Isaac
Watts, or any others of those many exemplary
Christians *whose bodies are buried in peace, but whose
names live for evermore**.

In every situation of life which appears parallel
to theirs, he will ask himself how they would have
acted, and he will find an answer by observing how
they really did act. Two or three such models will
furnish precedents which, with a little adaptation
to modern times, will afford a directory for conduct,
under all emergences. Great judgment is certainly
necessary even here; and I have already said, that
a blind imitation of any model whatever is not to
be approved.

Some have recommended not only the imitation
of a person of excellent character, but the habit of
supposing him *always present*, seeing and hearing us
on all occasions. We may thus make him our privy
counsellor, ask ourselves what he would say on such
a point, what advice he would give, and whether we
should be ashamed to act as our inclination prompts
us in his real presence. Thus he may become the
guide of our lives, and the regulator of our behaviour.

What I have said of a clergyman's choosing a
model may be applied to all other professions, and
indeed to all occupations, from the king to the me-

* Ecclesiasticus.

chanic. A good model once chosen will lead them in the journey of life as a hand-post directs the traveller over a wide waste or forest, or as the lamp from the beacon guides the mariner on the ocean. They must still use their own discernment, and exert their own efforts, or they may lose their way, even in full view of Eddystone lighthouse.

Civil or general history has always been extolled as the great teacher of wisdom. But its lessons are chiefly political, and kings and statesmen are principally concerned in them. *Biography* is the species of history best adapted to teach wisdom in private life. There are many lives of English worthies, which cannot be attentively read by an ingenuous young man, without exciting an ardour of virtue.

But living models may be also very advantageously selected by the aspirant after excellence. The danger is, lest the choice should fall on a wrong character. Splendour of rank, riches, honours, station, are too apt to recommend patterns which exhibit only a vicious exemplar, whitened and gilded by the hand of fashion. Envy and prejudice are also prone to add deformity to characters really beautiful. So that the choice of living examples is more difficult than that of the departed, whose fame is fixed by death.

But, so long as a good model is chosen, there is little doubt but that the means of arriving at excellence will be facilitated, whether the choice fall on the living, or on those who are out of the reach of envy.

The precept of Quintilian in the art of rhetoric must be observed in life. At first, and for a long time, only the best writers, and such as will not mislead him who implicitly confides in them, must be selected for imitation*.

---

* Diu non nisi optimus quisque, et qui credentem, sibi minimè fallat, legendus est.

But let not the imitation even of the best authors or the best men become a plagiarism either in writing or in life.   There is a noble *originality*, the characteristic of genius and the parent of all excellence.

————

NUMBER XXII.

On Dr. Johnson's Prayers, with a Remark on his Style.—Ev. 22.

THE greater part of those writers who have lately arrived at any very distinguished degree of fame, have favoured the cause of infidelity.   It is therefore the more pleasing to the friend of revelation and of mankind, to observe one of the most popular authors of our own country, and one of the ablest men that ever existed, zealously religious.   Every one had heard that Dr. Johnson was devout; but I believe, few entertained an adequate idea of his warmth and scrupulous regularity in the offices of devotion, till the publication of his Prayers and Meditations.

They exhibit the writer in a light in which he has seldom appeared to his readers.   He usually puts on a garb of dignity and command.   His Rambler is written in the style of authority.   His Prefaces to the Poets are dictatorial.   The reader is easily induced to believe that pride is a striking feature in his character.   But he no sooner opens the book of Prayers and Meditations, than he sees him in a state of true humility.   No affectation in the style.   No words of unusual occurrence.   Every expression is such as is well adapted to a frail mortal, however improved by art or favoured by nature, when he approaches the mercy-seat of the Almighty.

The reader is thus in some degree gratified, by observing a man, who had always appeared to him as a superior mortal, and exempt from human infirmities, feeling and acknowledging, with all humility, the common weaknesses of all human creatures.

It would be the partiality of prejudice to affirm, that the volume which I am now considering is free from all marks of superstition. To be uneasy because one has, through mistake, drank a spoonful of milk in a cup of tea on a fast day, argues a mind not entirely under the regulation of right reason. To pray for the dead is, I think, at least venial; but I am apprehensive that it will subject the devotee to the charge of superstition among the strict and severe in doctrinal religion.

Upon the whole, though there are many apparent weaknesses in the volume, which render it a cause of wonder, debate, and offence among many, yet it does honour to the writer of it, as a proof of remarkable piety. And with respect to weaknesses, alas! what is man but a complication of them? And indeed, who shall presume to determine decisively that the eccentricities of this book are weaknesses? Many of those who censure them as such, are probably far less capable of judging than Johnson, to whom they certainly did not appear in that light.

If he was sincere, and there is every reason to believe it, the most scrupulous particulars in the performance of his religious duties deserve a name far more honourable than that of acts of superstition. Man is a most wretched being unassisted by the protection of divine favour; how can it then be wondered that he is ready to attend to the minutest circumstance which, in the hour of distress, appears likely to secure it?

Before we condemn Johnson, let us examine our own conduct, and consider whether the confidence in which many of us live, and our neglect of religion, is not a *weakness* more deplorable than any thing in what is called the superstition of this pious man.

While I am speaking of Johnson, I cannot refrain from adding an observation on his style. It always appeared to me, and I believe is now generally thought, that he had selected Sir Thomas Brown as his model of style in the composition of the Rambler.

I select a few phrases from the *Vulgar Errors* of Brown in confirmation of my opinion.

' Intellectual acquisition is but reminiscential evocation.'

' We hope it will not be unconsidered that we find no constant manuduction in this labyrinth.'

' For not attaining the deuteroscopy, they are fain to omit the superconsequences, coherences, figures, or tropologies, and are not some time persuaded by fire beyond their literalities.'

' Their individual imperfections being great, they are moreover enlarged by their aggregation.'

' A faraginious concurrence of all conditions.'

' Being divided from truth themselves, they are yet farther removed by advenient deception.'

' Deluding their apprehension with ariolation.'

These passages I have selected, not because they are the most striking, but because they first occurred. A thousand instances of similarity might be produced, if the whole volume were searched, and if the limits of my paper would admit them.

Though Brown is an excellent writer, yet it must be allowed that he is pedantic ; and that he preferred polysyllabic expressions derived from the language of ancient Rome, to his vernacular vocabulary, even in instances where it was equally elegant and significant. Had he sought the fountains of antiquity only when those of his own times were dry, he would have deserved esteem for enriching the English language, and he might have been justly held up as an example for imitation; but he appears to use singular and magnificent words from ostentatious motives; and what, after all, does the use of them prove? That he was acquainted with the Latin and Greek languages, and that he was a learned etymologist. Sensible readers are not persuaded of another's general learning, or solid wisdom, by the pomp of exotic language.

But, notwithstanding this censure, Brown must be acknowledged to have contributed much to the *copia verborum*, by introducing words which in his age were uncouth, but which are now become elegant and familiar. Johnson, considered as a lexicographer and improver of the English language, did right to select an author for imitation, who presented him with a model for coining new words. Perhaps he was led to study Brown, among others, in order to qualify himself for the compilation of his lexicon, and in studying him, for this purpose, caught his style; but, after all, it is certain that his moral writing would have been more extended, and consequently done more service, had he chosen a style more simple, and less obscured to vulgar readers, by polysyllabic words of Latin and Greek etymology.

NUMBER XXIII.

On Long Prayers, and on the Devotions of Bishop Andrews.—Ev. 23.

'GIVE me,' said an ancient, 'whatever may be good for me, though I should neglect to pray for it; and deny me whatever may be hurtful, though I should ignorantly make it the object of my supplications.'

This may be called a laconic prayer. It has always been much admired. The perfect resignation to the Divine Will which it implies, renders it a model for the imitation of Christian piety.

Our Saviour himself seems to have disapproved of long prayers; and the invaluable prayer which he has condescended to dictate to erring mortals, is remarkable for its beautiful brevity. It might have been reasonably supposed, that the pious composers of prayers would have been desirous of imitating their great Master, in the conciseness of their petitionary compositions. But diffusion and repetition have been one of their most conspicuous blemishes. There is no doubt but that the practice which prevails among some respectable sects, of filling up a long portion of time in their public service with extemporary prayer, has contributed greatly to increase the length of prayers, beyond the limits both of reason and of sincere and attentive devotion.

The human mind is so formed as not to be able to retain any sentiment during a long time in a great degree of fervour. But prayer without fervour is, I fear, an unacceptable service. And this is the reason why brevity in prayer is expressly approved by Him, to whom prayer is to be offered, and who consequently must know what is most agreeable to himself, and what sort of service is the most expressive of man's sincerity.

The greater part of the English liturgy is very justly admired, as furnishing a fine example of supplicatory composition. The collects are remarkably excellent both for conciseness and fervour of expression. But it may be doubted, whether the whole of the service, comprehending three parts, intended at first to be separately used, is not longer than can be attended to devoutly even by the best disposed. The composition of most of the prayers is so well adapted to human wants and infirmities, that it might perhaps supersede the necessity of any other prayers, were it not found that the frequency of their use diminishes considerably the warmth and seriousness which otherwise they are calculated to inspire.

Books of prayers composed for private devotion are therefore very useful; and they are certainly not to be examined with great severity of criticism. But there is a little volume, entitled, Devotions of Bishop Andrews, translated from the Greek by Dean Stanhope, which lately attracted my particular attention, as my expectations were raised to an uncommon height by the following passage in the Preface:—

'The heart, already enlightened and inflamed with piety and charity, will here find something exactly suitable to its inward motions, and the *most significant and beautiful words* wherein to utter its holy desires, and those gracious sentiments which, without this help, would perhaps break forth *with less accuracy both of method and expression.* . . . . But the less perfect Christian, who has not yet made so much progress in the school of piety as the former, may reap still greater benefit from this work. It will tend to improve him in *knowledge and practice.* . . . . Indeed what less can be expected, when a book of this nature is composed of materials taken out of the Holy Scriptures, and very ancient liturgies, which bear the names of St. James, St. Basil, and St. Chrysostom, collected and put together by the most judicious workmen in this way; such as were the persons mentioned in the title-page, Dr. Andrews, once Bishop of Winchester, and Dr. Stanhope, late Dean of Canterbury.'

After reading these and other passages in the Preface, which are equally strong in the praises of this little manual, it will not be thought extraordinary, that I took up the book with great avidity. I admired the pious strain of some of it; but I could not help thinking that the valuable parts of it are disgraced by some passages almost ridiculous. I transcribe the following from the close of ' An Act of Faith for Friday.'

' O, dearest Saviour, impart to me thy whole self; and let every part and act of thine have its saving influence over me.

' Sanctify me by thy Spirit; feed and strengthen me by thy body; ransom me by thy blood; *wash me in thy water;* heal me by thy stripes; *refresh me with thy sweat;* hide me in thy wounds.'

I take the liberty of asking any candid reader, whether such petitions are the natural effusions of sincere devotion; whether they are not rather of a trifling and whimsical turn; and whether they do not open a door for the scorner? ' Let us pray with the spirit, but let us pray with the understanding also.'

I know it will be said, that while a form of prayer gives no offence to the simple and well-meaning devotee, for whom it was chiefly designed, it is a matter of little moment whether it please or displease the fastidious critic and the captious wit. But to this I must reply, that it is certainly of importance, not to furnish, in any religious composition, real occasion either for censure or derision; and I might add, that it appears to be an affront to the Majesty of heaven, to offer up a petition to God in a style and manner in which we should be ashamed to address an earthly potentate. A trifling, a quibbling, a nonsensical, prayer can never be the production of a mind warmed with a devotion at once rational and sincere.

I presume not to censure the editor, whom I consider as one of the best ornaments of our church. The blemishes of this little book came not from him, I venture to affirm, but from Dean Stanhope, from Bishop Andrews, or from some older writer. I have no copy of the original, and cannot therefore discover whether the above prayer is faithfully translated from it. But I think it cannot proceed from Dr. Horne, whose judgment and beautiful style in the expression of devotional feelings, I have often admired.

The language of a prayer should be natural and warm from the heart, yet at the same time restrained and chastised by good sense, otherwise it must degenerate to the nonsense of the dotard, or the madness of the enthusiast. Dr. Johnson deserves great praise for the simplicity and energy of many of his prayers. Nothing of his pompous style, his long words, or formal periods, is to be observed in them. His good understanding suggested to him the impropriety of all affectation, when he laid aside all pretensions to wisdom, and with a humility, which must always become the greatest of mortals, approached the throne of the Almighty.

After all that taste and criticism can suggest, it is certain that uprightness of intention and fervent piety are the best beauties of supplicatory writings. He to whom prayer is addressed, considers not the form of words, and the structure of periods; but the faith, the sincerity, the charity of the poor petitioner. If the heart be right, the errors of the understanding and of the lips will pass unnoticed. Yet it is decent and reasonable to take care, according to the best of our knowledge, not to offer up prayers in which there is any known defect unworthy a creature furnished by the Creator with those intellectual powers, which surely can never be more honour-

ably exerted than in the service of Him who gave
them.

'I use not to run rashly into prayer,' says Howell,
'without a trembling precedent meditation; and if
any odd thoughts intervene and grow upon me, I
check myself and recommence; and this is incident
to long prayers, which are more subject to man's
weakness and the devil's malice.'

NUMBER XXIV.

*On reading trifling uninstructive Books, called Summer
Reading.*—Ev. 24.

Belli libelli, lepidi, novi libelli.—IGNORAMUS.

'SIR,

'As I came to this water-drinking place to relax
myself from the fatigues of a profession which requires great application and confinement, I am resolved to make use of all the methods which an ingenious and polite place has invented for the valuable purpose of killing time. Accustomed to reading
as I have always been, I cannot omit books, while I
seek the means of amusement; but I am forbidden
by my physician to read any thing but what is called
summer reading, and therefore I am a frequent
lounger at the circulating library. By the way, I
beg leave to give you a hint, that if you do not con-
trive to make your Winter Evenings summer reading, they will not be much noticed in the repository of knowledge, where I am now writing you this
letter.

'As I often sit and read in the library, I have an

opportunity of hearing what books are in the most request; and I am frequently not a little diverted with observing the great eagerness with which tomes, totally unknown to me, who have made books the study of my life, are demanded of the librarian. The first question on entering the shop I found to be universally.—Have you any thing new? I should have supposed that the publications of the last year would have deserved this epithet; but I found by observation that scarcely any thing is esteemed new, but what is just advertised, and almost wet from the press. Curiosity seems to be the great stimulus of the subscribers; idle curiosity, as I may call it, since it seems to seek its own gratification independently of all desire of increasing the store of knowledge, improving the taste, or confirming the principles.

'I have smiled at hearing a lady admire the delicacy of sentiment which the author of some novel, which she had just been reading, must possess; though I knew it to be the production of some poor hireling, destitute of learning and taste, knowledge of life and manners, and furnished with the few ideas he had by reading the novels of a few preceding years. He had inserted in the title-page, By a Lady; and various conjectures were often hazarded, in my hearing, concerning the authoress. Some hinted that they were acquainted with her, and that it was a lady of quality. Others knew it to be written by an acquaintance of their own; while all agreed in asserting, it must be by a lady, the sentiments were so characteristically delicate and refined. You may conjecture how much I was disposed to laugh when I was informed that it was the production of a hackney scribbler in Black-Boy-alley.

'I confess I had been much more conversant in a college library than in a circulating one, and could not therefore but be astonished at the number of volumes which the students would devour. The *Helluo Librorum*, or Glutton of Books, was a character well known at the university, and mentioned by the ancients; but I believe their idea of him is far exceeded by many a fair subscriber at the circulating library. I have known a lady read twenty volumes in a week during two or three months successively. To be sure they were not bulky tomes, such as those of which it was predicated that a great book was a great evil. The print in the pages of most of them, to speak in the mechanical style of mensuration, were three inches by one and a half, and the blank paper exceeded the printed in quantity by at least one moiety on a moderate computation.

'Now, Sir, I am not one of those who mean austerely to censure this mode of reading; for I am of opinion that it is often very innocent, and sometimes not without considerable advantage. There are certainly many novels which, though little known in the literary world, are not without merit, and of a very virtuous tendency. Most of them tend to recommend benevolence and liberality; for it is the fashion of the age to affect those qualities; and I really think, as conversation is usually conducted, scarcely so many opportunities occur of imbibing benevolent and virtuous sentiments from it, as from the decent books of a circulating library: I say decent, for I am sorry to observe, that in the multitude of new books which the librarians are obliged to purchase, some have a tendency to diffuse every kind of evil which can mislead the understanding and corrupt the heart.

'The danger of indiscriminately reading whatever has the recommendation of novelty, induced me to take up my pen and write to you, hoping that I might suggest a caution on the subject to some of your fair readers, who, I am sure, have recourse to a circulating library solely to improve and amuse themselves while under the hair-dresser's operation.

'They would, I think, do right to inquire the character of every book they read, before they take it into their dressing-room, and to shew the same caution in the choice of their circulating-library books, as they would in the selection of their company.

Yours, &c.   SENEX.'

NUMBER XXV.

On being disgusted with Bashfulness in Boys.—Ev. 25.

To prevent the evil which arises from attempting things beyond their strength, nature seems to have given many animals that instinctive knowledge of their want of ability which produces caution. The bird, while it is callow, never leaves the nest, unless by an accidental fall; and when its plumage is grown to a considerable degree of perfection, it takes but short flights at a time, and seems unwilling to lose sight of its parent and nurse. It is not till the wings have acquired strength and agility that it leaves the branches or the ground, and dares to soar undauntedly in the fields of air, unmindful of the nest and the fostering feathers, which lately supplied it with warmth and protection.

Something of a similar diffidence, arising from conscious immaturity of power, appears to me to take place in the human mind at the puerile age; and I cannot help thinking it truly amiable; yet it is stigmatized with the odious name of shyness and sheepishness, and many parents appear more solicit-

ous to divest their children of it, than to furnish them
with any grace, virtue, or accomplishment. By dint
of great pains, they often succeed in thus forcing
the rose-bud to expand its immature leaves; but I
fear they are greatly mistaken in their management,
and that their uneasiness at seeing their children
diffident is totally misplaced.

If indeed the diffidence, which they lament, were
likely to continue through life, I agree with them
that it would be a great misfortune. It would prevent exertion, in a thousand instances, where exertion would be rewarded with profit and honour; and
it would occasion the child much causeless anxiety.
But in general, there is no danger of its continuance
beyond the period of immaturity, at which it is certainly natural, and rather pleasing and graceful, in
the eyes of sensible observers. I contend that it is
caused by conscious inability arising from youth,
and that it will of itself give place to a proper confidence, as soon as it feels a consciousness of power
matured and confirmed by age.

I believe I may go farther, and assert that this
unfashionable diffidence, which many fathers and
mothers labour to remove, even in the tender period
of early infancy, is favourable to growth in mental
vigour and virtuous principles. All who are to excel
in future must devote a previous time to discipline.
He who would one day speak must first listen. And,
to return to the bird, to which I have already al-
luded, it is well known to the students in ornitho-
logy, or at least to those admirers of the feathered
race called bird-fanciers, that the finest singing-birds
listen when young to the old ones, and even when
they have learned their notes, venture only to *record*,
as those gentlemen express it, that is, to sing in a
soft low tone, almost as if they were ashamed of
being heard. I have often heard the blackbird, who

has afterward made the woods resound with his melody, trying his skill, or *recording*, under the covert of a hawthorn, in so low a warbling, as scarcely to be distinguished amid the concert of the grove.

The mind collects images of things, and forms opinions during the immature state, at which it scarcely ventures to employ the tongue in utterance. And when a store of ideas is at last accumulated, it feels a spontaneous confidence founded on conscious merit; and shines, at a mature age, with a lustre which it would never have displayed, if, instead of collecting ideas, it had been indulging its own pride in uttering vivacious nonsense.

I am of opinion that men of the greatest genius, of fine imagination and sensibility, were of necessity timid and diffident in the puerile period; and I wish parents not to infer, from the diffidence and silence of their children, that they are naturally stupid. There is indeed an appearance of diffidence which arises from real dulness; but there is a real diffidence caused by excess of sensibility, and it is a favourable presage of all that is lovely and excellent in human nature. Parents will therefore endeavour to discriminate duly, before they decide on the abilities of their children, from the appearance of timidity or shyness in company, and their diffidence in saying or doing any thing which their age has not afforded them opportunities to learn. They will be cautious of removing this veil which nature furnishes for defect, as she guards the blossom before it has acquired strength sufficient to admit of full expansion. If the bud, which would naturally expand in April or May, were rudely opened in March, what fruit could justly be expected in August and September?

Nothing is more common than to observe parents introducing a boy of eight or nine years old into company, to balls, and to assemblies, with the professed intention of wearing off that sheepishness (for such is the ignominious term) which he may have unfortunately contracted at school or in the nursery. Neither is he suffered to be silent, lest his friends should attribute silence to dulness. Contrary to his inclination, the poor boy must force himself to be pert and loquacious to all whom he encounters, or he will be ridiculed and reproached for stupidity. Unfortunate mistake! If he should become a proficient at this early age, in the school of audacity, to what a height of impudence will he arrive in manhood? of impudence unsupported by knowledge, or any real merit, which can justify even confidence. Too many in this age, are trained in this mistaken plan, which is the reason why we commonly meet with forward young men, who overpower all around them with noise, who are incapable of rational conversation, who are avoided by all sensible persons, and who associate with the only characters, who can enjoy their company, gamesters, horse-jockeys, phaeton-drivers, drunkards, and debauchees. Their mistaken parents succeeded too well in divesting them at an early age, of that diffidence which was natural, which was becoming, and which would have been the means of preserving their innocence, their characters, their health, their fortune, every thing by which life is honourably embellished, and death rendered less formidable.

NUMBER XXVI.

On the Effect of ancient and modern Music.—Ev. 26.

IF a general ardour of a whole people in the pursuit of excellence be likely to obtain it in its highest degree, it might reasonably be expected that the English nation should at this time be singularly distinguished for a skill in music. The musical mania, if it may be so called, has diffused itself from the court to the cottage, from the orchestra of royal theatres, to the rustics in the gallery of a country church. As Juvenal said of the Greeks of his time who migrated to Rome for interest, that it was a nation of comedians, we may say of the English, that they are a nation of musicians.

But has this general ardour produced that stupendous, unexampled, excellence which might have been expected? I allow the effect only to be an adequate criterion of that excellence. And what is the usual effect of a concert? It is in general an admiration of the performers, of the skill in execution, the volubility of singers, the quickness of the eye, and the delicacy of the ear. But how are the passions affected? Look round the room and see the index of the passions, the eyes and the countenances of the audience. Smiles and complacent looks abound; but these are no indications of those sudden transitions of violent emotion, which music is said to have charms sufficiently to excite. A few may sometimes appear *affected;* but there is reason to suspect that it is too often an *affectation,* not the most laudable or amiable.

Among the ancients the effects of music are said

to have been almost miraculous. The celebrated Ode of Dryden has made every one acquainted with the magic power of Timotheus over the emotions of the human heart. And all, who have read any thing of ancient history, must have remarked the wonderful effects attributed to the musical instrument in the hand of a master.

Among a hundred other stories, which evince the power of music, I recollect the following: Pythagoras was once likely to be troubled at his lecture, by a company of young men, inflamed with wine, and petulant with the natural insolence of youthful levity. The philosopher wished to repress their turbulence; but forbore to address them in the language of philosophy, which they would either not have attended to, or have treated with derision. He said nothing, but ordered the musician to play a grave majestic tune of the Doric style. The effect was powerful and instantaneous. The young men were brought to their sober senses, were ashamed of their wanton behaviour, and with one accord tore off the chaplets of flowers, with which they had decorated their temples in the hour of convivial gaiety. They listened to the philosopher. Their hearts were opened to instruction by music, and the powerful impression being well-timed, produced in them a permanent reformation.

How desirable is it to revive the music of Pythagoras! How concise a method of philosophizing to the purpose! What sermon or moral lecture would have produced a similar effect so suddenly?

But nothing of this kind was ever produced by the most successful efforts of modern music. Let us suppose a case somewhat similar to the preceding. Let us imagine a number of intoxicated rakes entering the theatre with a professed intention to cause a riot. Such a case has often been real. The music in the orchestra has done all that it could do to soothe the growing rage; but it was as impotent and contemptible as a pistol against a battery. It would be a fine thing for the proprietors, if a tune or two could save the benches, and the fiddlers preclude the carpenters. But Timotheus and the Doric strains are no more; yet surely, in so general a study of music, it might be expected that something of their perfection might be revived.

'That the music of the ancients,' says Jeremy Collier, ' could command farther than the modern, is past dispute. Whether they were masters of a greater compass of notes, or knew the secret of varying them more artificially; whether they *adjusted the intervals of silence more exactly*, had their hands or their voices farther improved, or their instruments better contrived; whether they had a deeper insight into the philosophy of nature, or understood the laws of the union of the soul and body more thoroughly; and thence were enabled to touch the passions, strengthen the sense, or prepare the medium, with greater advantage; whether they excelled us in all, or in how many of these ways, is not so clear; however, this is certain, that our improvements in this kind are little better than *ale-house crowds* (fiddles) with respect to theirs.'

I must leave it to the Burneys and the Bateses of the age to determine to what cause the little effect of music on the passions is to be ascribed. In reviving and performing the works of Handel, they have done much towards vindicating the declining honours of impassioned music. But still the commanding effect recorded by antiquity seems to remain a great desideratum.

I profess to consider the subject not as a musician, but as a moralist; in which character, I cannot help wishing to find that sort of music cultivated, which possesses an empire over the heart, and which, like oil poured on the troubled waves of the sea, can soothe the tumultuous passions to tranquillity. I wish to see the musician, who not only pleases my ear by his sounds, and delights my eye by his legerdemain, but who, in the words of Horace, *irritat, mulcet,* enrages or stills my emotions at his discretion. I wish to hear musical Shakspeares and Miltons touch the lyre, or inspire the tube.

I should have ventured to conclude, from the universal application to music, from the perfection of the instruments, and the ingenuity of the compositions, that the art is at this time arrived at its ultimate excellence. It is not easy to conceive, that much more can be done; and I am very doubtful whether the ancients had equal excellence in theory or in execution. Yet, after all, when I consider the effect, I am compelled, however reluctantly, to deplore the great inferiority of the modern to ancient music. As I am no artist on the pipe or on the lyre, I can only suspect that the defect arises from the want of simplicity. It may not, after all, be unjust to surmise that the accounts handed down of the stupendous effects of music among the Greeks are exaggerated by *Græcia mendax,* or that disposition of ancient Greece to fiction, which gave rise to the nonsense of mythology.

NUMBER XXVII.

*On the Effect of Caricatures exhibited at the Windows
of Printsellers.*—Ev. 27.

Animum pictura pàscis.—VIRG.

POISON may be converted into medicine; and ridicule, which, when directed against morality and religion, operates like a pestilence, may be used to
expose vice and folly with peculiar efficacy.

The mode of ridiculing by prints has some advantages over that by writing and argument. Its effect
is instantaneous; and they who cannot read, or have
not sense enough to comprehend, a refined piece of
raillery, are able to see a good caricatura, and to
receive a powerful impression from it.

The lower classes in London, it may be supposed,
have not time, inclination, or ability, to read much,
but their minds are filled with ideas, not only by the
multitude of occurrences, but also by the prints which
are obtruded on their notice, in the windows of shops
conspicuously situated in the most frequented streets.
And, I believe, they often receive impressions either
favourable, or unfavourable, to their honesty and
happiness, as they loiter at a window, with a burden
on their backs, and gape, unmindful of their toil, at
the comical productions of the ingenious designer.
Every benevolent man must wish, that whatever representations have a tendency to corrupt and mislead them, might be kept out of sight; and only such
exhibited in the window, as may divert them innocently, or convey some useful instruction. I say
nothing on the subject of indecent prints at present,

as every one must acknowledge that they infuse a poison, the bad effects of which none can trace to their ultimate malignity.

But it appears to me, that the exhibition of the first magistrate, and of great statesmen, in caricatura, must contribute to diminish or destroy that reverence, which is always due to legal authority and established rank, and which is confessedly conducive to the most valuable ends of human society. The virulence of party hesitates not to represent royalty itself in situations, which must render it contemptible in the eyes of kennel-rakers, shoe-blackers, chimney-sweepers, and beggars. Their contempt, it will be said, is of little consequence, and yet these personages made their power felt in the memorable month of June, 1780; and riot and disorder are greatly promoted by emancipating them from all reverence for their superiors; and how can they respect the subordinate dignities, who are taught to defile the fountain of honour, and to malign the author of all civil dignity? Besides, the effect is by no means confined to their order. The contempt must have been diffused through the higher and middle ranks, before it descended to them; and there is great reason to believe, that the turbulent opposition to authority, which has disgraced the present reign, originated and grew from the contempt thrown on the higher orders by various methods, and, among others, by ludicrous representation on the copper-plate.

Our laws have been careful of the reputation of the subject, and libels cannot be published without the peril of a prosecution. But the framers of the laws did not perhaps foresee, that the engraver, as well as the writer, might be guilty of defamation, and would deserve to be restrained by the terrors, and the penalties of legal control. Our love of liberty is so ardent, that, like other violent passions, it overshoots its mark, and loses the object at which it aims. Else a practice which infringes on private liberty, more than any act of any king in this country, could not be suffered to prevail without restraint, and with triumphant impunity. What can savour more of the oppression of wanton tyranny than not to permit a man to be ugly in his person without exhibiting him as a spectacle and a laughing-stock, in the streets of the great city? Is a man to be put to shame, to stand, as it were, in the pillory, a mark for scorn to point her finger at, because nature has given him a long nose, a protuberant belly, or an ill-shapen leg?

Indeed, of all satire, none is so ungenerous, as that which reflects on personal deformity, one of the principal of the τα ουκ φ' ημι, *the things which are not in our own power*, and for which we are often no more accountable than for bad weather, pestilential blasts, or inundations. But the inventors of caricatures are not contented with representing the deformity, as it really exists, but glory in their ability to add to distortion, and render an irregularity, or defect, which would pass unnoticed, eminently and ridiculously conspicuous. A man of sense and fortitude, it will be said, may despise a contempt, which arises from circumstances, for which he cannot be blamed; but is the very person, who urges this, possessed of such sense, and such fortitude, as to despise any kind of ridicule which will adhere to him, as a stigma of reproach? With all our pretensions to wisdom, there are none but those who have lost their sensibility, who can patiently bear to become objects of public derision, either for singularities of the mind, or the body.

The practice of exhibiting all persons of consequence, in caricature, may therefore not only injure the public, by diminishing the respect due to official authority, but cruelly invade the peace of families, and distress the bosom of an unoffending individual. It deserves, then, to be reprobated, by all good and thinking men, who are unwilling to sacrifice, for the sake of a laugh, public welfare, and private tranquillity.

Ridicule has been always supposed peculiarly injurious, as it is confessedly indecent, in the affairs of religion. I believe wisdom will always be justified by her children, and that Christianity is founded on a rock so firmly, that the gates of hell shall not prevail against it; but yet, I am convinced, that to treat its ministers or ordinances with contempt, may do it great injury among the lower orders and weak minds, who will be thus led to despise what cannot be despised with safety. There are few subjects which the designers of ludicrous prints take more delight in, than to represent clergymen in a laughable situation and figure. I mention one instance of a print, which would hardly deserve notice, if it had not become popular among the vulgar. The print of the Vicar and Moses is often hung up on the walls of the farmhouse, where the clergyman of the parish used to be reverenced as a saint, and consequently was able to do great good; but is it to be supposed that this reverence will not be diminished, among the children at least, who from their infancy are accustomed to behold the parson an object of derision, a glutton, and a drunkard?

Any mode of affording innocent diversion, of exciting mirth without giving pain, is not only allowable, but desirable, in a world abounding with evil, and in a state of existence, which is, of necessity, burdened with care. But all human things require limitations. The genius of a Hogarth is certainly worthy of admiration, as an excellence; and of honour, as having been made a vehicle of great good to society. Hogarth finely moralized his pencil. His imitators have not reached his excellence in art, they have scarcely aimed at his morality, but they have abused their petty talents in lowering every thing great and venerable.

Some late designers in caricatura have merit; and if they would confine their ridicule to vice and villany, they would add to the praise which is due to them, as men of skill and genius, that which is superior, the praise of benevolence, and the virtue of doing good in their generation.

Many may be disposed to consider ludicrous prints as trifles; but apparent trifles are acknowledged by all wise men to lead to serious evils, and they ought to be carefully suppressed, while they continue trifles, and while the suppression is therefore practicable. Every good member of society must acknowledge the value of decency, good order, public tranquillity, and private security; and every sensible and observing man may observe, that all these may be destroyed by the libels of the pencil. No one knows whose turn it may be to suffer next, and it is therefore the interest of all, even of the perpetrators of the mischief themselves, to discourage the prevalence of wanton assassination.

NUMBER XXVIII.

On modern Heroism.—Ev. 28.

It is said by the learned, that the age of heroism is no more; but I beg leave to dissent from their opinion. An age, I suppose, derives that appellation from its abundance of heroes. If so, then the present age may be styled heroic. I cannot say that we have many Alexanders, Cæsars, and Charleses; but, if what the world call spirit, fire, and genius, constitute a hero, we certainly abound in heroes.

The name, indeed, *hero*, is not usually adopted, because it is become a little unfashionable. But the character exists at present under the title of a DASH-ING FELLOW.

The etymology of the word *dashing*, is doubtful; but among other explanations of its meaning, our lexicographer says it signifies, ' to fly off in *flashes* with a loud noise.' In this sense, it is very applicable to the character of the true dashing fellow.

The object of this kind of hero, is fame, or rather distinction. He scorns inglorious ease, though accompanied with health, plenty, and the esteem of his acquaintance. Health, plenty, and esteem, what are ye to public renown? Think of the bliss of being admired at a horse-race, pointed at in a theatre, and daily celebrated in the paragraphs of a *dashing* newspaper.

The dashing fellow, as great genius usually shews strong indications of it at the earliest age, begins his career of glory at the public school, to which he is sent by his parents, to rub off the shyness incident to natural modesty and the immaturity of youth. At school, he scorns to pore over musty Greek and Latin, but gloriously aims at being pre-eminent in every mischievous frolic, scorning the control of his master, and taking the lead in every attempt to revolt against authority, and in support of liberty, ' that goddess heavenly bright.' He spends his money, with which he is plentifully furnished by his parents on purpose to *distinguish* him, not in boyish gratifications, but in hiring horses, keeping pointers and terriers, giving dinners, and in every noble enterprise of vice and wantonness, of which his age is capable.

On leaving school, whence he has deserved the honour of expulsion a thousand times, though the grovelling spirit of the master would not confer it, he aspires at the splendid distinctions of the turf, the gaming-table, and the whip ; not to mention his illustrious emulation of the Grand Seignior in the establishment of his seraglio.

If he is born to a large estate, he disdains to wait, like meaner spirits, for the death of those on whom it depends, or till he comes to age, but munificently bestows premiums on the despised Israelites, to supply his present unconfined generosity. And though he should borrow and spend more than he will be ever able to repay, he is above stooping to the narrow thoughts of pecuniary concerns. With an heroic confidence he trusts for future supplies to time, to fortune, to the friendly dice, to any thing, and to nothing.

Thus furnished with money, the sinews of heroism as well as war, he sallies forth in quest of adventures in a high car, ycleped a phaeton, drawn by six steeds, not bigger than ponies, but beautiful enough to attract all eyes, at every inn, and through every town he passes, in his rapid progress from horse-race to horse-race. The importance of his objects renders an unparalleled expedition sometimes so necessary, that he condescends to hire hack-horses, an inglorious measure, if some lustre were not to be reflected on it, by killing three or four of them in their harnesses, that he may reach the race-ground at the moment of starting from the goal. Fame blows her trumpet through all the country immediately, and the newspapers re-echo the report on the morrow, that young Dashwell travelled all night to reach Newmarket, and killed six horses on the road: glorious achievement, worthy to be recorded in the temple of fame, in letters of gold, on pillars of brass!

Arrived at the race-ground, he distinguishes himself more than any of the paltry fellows at the Olympian and Pythian games, so celebrated by the Theban. He clothes himself in a leathern cap, a short waistcoat, long buckskin small-clothes, and the neatest boots and spurs!—mounts the racer, and rides the race. If he dislocates his shoulder, or breaks his collar-bone, the little pain is despised, for the ample compensation of being generally talked of and renowned, as the best gentleman-jockey in the three kingdoms.

But distinctions like this are not sufficient for his great soul. He must fight a duel, before his claim to complete heroism, or *dashism,* can be universally allowed. Nothing more easy than to find an occasion. His best friend will furnish him with one over the next bottle of burgundy. He gives the lie direct; a challenge ensues; the parties meet; one fires without taking aim; the other, into the air; the seconds interfere; the duel is over, the account is drawn up, signed by the seconds, inserted in the morning papers, and the glory of both parties established on a basis never to be shaken. Dashwell's business is done, his name is up: he has taken a degree in glory; he was a dashing fellow before; he is now a d—d dashing fellow.

But to the ambitious, Alps on Alps are continually rising. He wishes to be renowned for his spirit at the gaming-table. He stakes the whole reversion of his estate, and loses it with a cool intrepidity that might shame the Catos and Reguluses of antiquity.

The bottle remains for consolation; and great are his achievements under the banners of Bacchus. But his health declines: his hands shake: his legs totter: he wants a wife as a nurse: he goes, in pursuit of one, into the regions of old Drury, and marries an Amazon as common as a hackney-coach. She becomes a termagant. His dashing spirit, unused to control, and above submission to the loss of fortune, health, and tranquillity, finishes the career of glory with a pistol.

But dashing fellows are not confined to high life. There are multitudes of gentlemen volunteers in this honourable service among the lower orders. Swindlers, forgers, coiners, and highwaymen, are all dashing fellows. But England, like Athens in this respect, is ungrateful to her great men. As the Athenians banished their distinguished worthies by the ostracism, so the English send their heroes into exile by the rigour of their laws. Botany-bay is colonized by dashing young fellows; and multitudes are now riding in phaetons, galloping fiery steeds, and living in style, as it is called, on purpose to qualify themselves, on some future day, for this honourable dismission from their native country.

Even the literary community is not without its share of dashing fellows. They chiefly appear in the form of political pamphleteers, paragraph writers, hand-bill authors, and *philosophers of a liberal way of thinking*. One writes a pamphlet full of treason and abuse of his majesty, that attracts notice for a day, and immediately thinks himself a second Solon. Another scribbles a paltry ode, or poem, in which he asperses with filth and venom the king, and all other virtuous characters, and immediately rises in his own estimation to the rank of a Swift or a Butler. A third scribbles quaint paragraphs that would disgrace a chambermaid, so destitute are they of common sense and composition, and then deems himself the wittiest and merriest wight in all Christendom. A fourth, being a philosopher, aims a deadly stroke at Christianity, and rises in his own eyes a polemical Goliath, though the first stone in the sling of a true man, with no higher pretensions than to common sense and common honesty, brings him to the ground. All these are dashing fellows, great in their own opinion, and in the opinion of the little circle connected by similar principles and practices; but great as they appear, the community would feel itself relieved by their honourable banishment to Botany-bay, as the stomach is refreshed after the evacuation of an emetic.

These dashing characters may be compared to a dashing torrent, all noise, all foam, all violence, for a moment, and then spent and exhausted for ever; or to a comet, attracting all eyes for a short time, but cheering no system, and perhaps endangering all; or to a kettle-drum, which owes its power of making a noise to brass and emptiness; or to some vile liquors, hot in the mouth, but without a body.

A dashing fellow, indeed, however he may admire himself, or be gazed at by the public, displays so many symptoms of insanity, that, if his real friends were to put him on a straight waistcoat, feed him on bread and water, or take out a statute of lunacy against him, they might be justified by the circumstances, and would probably prevent much injury to himself and to the public.

It is greatly to be wished, that young men who are actuated by the perverse ambition of being *distinguished* for a conduct and qualities which are mischievous and irrational in the highest degree, would consider that *distinction* is then only honour, when it is founded on esteem; and that to be talked of, and stared at, for extravagance and folly, are but poor compensations for the loss of honour, fortune, health, peace, and life.

True heroism is best displayed by acting a ra-

tional, manly, uniform part; and by shewing sense
to despise the applause, and spirit to defy the sneers,
of fashionable folly, however it may be countenanced
by the example of the rich and the noble, by the favour of the great, and the patronage of the powerful. It is meanness and cowardice to yield reason
and right to ridicule. It is a spirit worthy of a man,
to proceed in the path of rectitude, under the guidance of principle, careless of undeserved censure,
and unsolicitous for the admiration of an unthinking
multitude. Contrasted with this, the false fire of
the *dashing* fellow is like the blaze of a handful of
straw compared to the undiminished radiance of the
vestal flame.

NUMBER XXIX.

*On the Art which has lately been honoured with the
name of Pugilism.*—Ev. 29.

HUMANE and considerate men cannot observe, without concern, the prevalence of a taste for any diversion which contributes to the degradation of human
nature. That the taste for boxing, unhappily revived in the present age, has such a tendency, cannot be doubted by those who duly reflect on the
principle from which it proceeds, and the consequences it tends to produce.

It originates in a ferocious disposition, and a
CONTEMPTUOUS OPINION OF MAN. No gentle
and benevolent mind can derive amusement and
delight from a spectacle, which must cause pain
and danger to those who exhibit it; and none but
those who consider man as an animal, not at all su-

perior to the beasts, can endeavour to engage two
fellow-creatures in a combat, which, in cool blood,
may cause the loss of limbs, and the loss of life.
Can he have any idea of the soul's immortality, of
man's being made a little lower than the angels,
and of the superintendence of the Deity, who views
with joy, approaching to ecstasy, two poor wretches
endeavouring to destroy each other for hire; who
makes it the principal business of his life to see such
sights, and to promote their frequent repetition;
who derives gain from them as well as pleasure, and
pursues them with the same ardour and constancy,
as others prosecute the study of an honourable profession? Such a taste must proceed from a gross
ignorance of better and more manly pleasures, and
from a savage heart, restrained only by human laws
from the actual perpetration of the worst cruelty.

The consequences of this taste, to individuals and
to society, are truly deplorable. When the combat
is announced, all the vilest members of the community are eager to partake in an amusement congenial
to their corrupted natures. The scene of action is
crowded with an assemblage of wretches, who conduct, under their triumphant banners, riot, intemperance, violence; who defy all civil order, all decency, every thing for which laws were enacted, and
society established. A successful example is given
of disobedience to law, which paves the way to anar-
chy, revolt, and rebellion. An insult is offered to
the civil magistracy, which those who encourage it
may hereafter rue, when they feel the consequent
depredations on their property, their persons, and
their peace.

The lower orders are taught to believe, what indeed they are at all times ready to suppose, that
there is an excellence, which the greatest men in the
nation may admire, in the exercise of a mere brute

force, in defeating their neighbour by violence, without equity ; and in striking a terror into the minds of the good and orderly, who are not endowed with muscular vigour and superior size. Government was instituted to protect the weak against the strong ; but the boxing rage contributes to increase the tendency of the strong to injure and oppress the weak.

It has been the scope of all who have laboured in the civilization of mankind, to soften the native ferocity of the human heart, to control its propensity to violence and cruelty, to infuse a spirit of mutual benevolence, and teach a willingness to leave the redress of private wrongs to public justice. But the boxing mania does all that can be done in the present enlightened times, to bring back man to his original barbarity, to ignorance, to selfishness, to injustice, to contempt of laws, to infringement of property, to every base and destructive action and inclination which the laws of God and man have uniformly prohibited.

But strongly as the lovers of law and order express themselves against this savage taste, there are not wanting men pretending to political wisdom, who advance arguments in its favour. Let what they have urged be fairly considered.

It is said, that the encouragement of boxing promotes a martial and a manly spirit among those whom the nation may one day call forth to supply her armies and her navies.

I believe it is not agreed that those who excel in muscular strength, or in the skill necessary to exert it in single combat, are superior to others in courage or conduct during the heat of action with a public enemy. A boxer, or a lover of boxing, is not a better soldier or sailor than the hardy husbandman or manufacturer. Superior strength or bulk is not required to pull a trigger, fire a cannon, or to climb up a rope. A fist, though tutored by the best *rules of science,*

Qualia vincant
Pythagoran Anytique reum—— HORAT.

avails little against a sword, a musket, or a bayonet, in the hands of a dwarf, or a man who never heard of the name or the art of a pugilist. And as to the manliness of spirit which boxing, and the love of it, are said to promote, is it not rather a proof of meanness, than manliness, to fight a man in cool blood, for *lucre,* and to afford amusement to those who pay for admission to the spectacle? Persons who did this, were always numbered among the meanest of mankind, and certainly have no right to be considered of nobler dispositions than tumblers, rope-dancers, riders of three horses, and fire-eaters, all whose pranks are attended with danger, voluntarily incurred for the sake of lucre.

To bear blows without regarding the pain, to inflict blows without feeling reluctance or compassion, argues, indeed, an insensibility of body and mind; but insensibility can never be deemed a perfection; can never produce that sort of courage which derives force from conduct, that sort of manliness which owes its value to its origin in reason. An attempt to reduce men merely to machines, in the hands of their superiors, is of so base and ungenerous a nature, that it ought to be reprobated by all who have any real manliness in their character.

The plough and the anvil, the axe and the hammer, will always supply a race of men with sinews strong enough to undergo all the hardships and labour of war; and the native sentiments of such a race, in a land of liberty, will always produce a spirit sufficiently manly, without encouraging any practices which are, of necessity, cruel and savage. Cruelty, of every kind and degree, has in it something inherently base and dastardly, and never can be compatible with real heroism. It may make a bully and an assassin, but neither a warrior nor a patriot.

It is also said, that boxing is the natural mode of terminating those disputes which will always arise in the collisions of human intercourse. I grant that in the savage state it may appear to be the natural mode of deciding quarrels; but England has long been in a state of high civilization; and they who, by any mode, endeavour to bring it back again to what is called the state of nature, must give up all pretensions to philosophy and wisdom, and deserve to be marked as the enemies, not only of their country, but of their species. I have heard it even denied that the fist is the natural instrument of attack and defence, since the hand is evidently formed to hold a weapon with greater effect, and since all nations, in the most uncultivated state, use weapons, from the *patoo patoo* of the South Sea islanders, to the broad sword of the British soldier. But this I only mention as matter of curious speculation; for the first being less offensive than the sword would be preferred by the philanthropist.

It is farther contended, that, allowing the boxers themselves to be a mean and pitiable race, their engagements furnish a manly and improving spectacle to gentlemen who have leisure to seek their own amusement from every thing that can afford it. That it is not a manly spectacle to behold two fellow-creatures injuring each other as much as they can, by brute force, is, I think, evident from what has been already said; and that it is not an improving spectacle, is equally clear, if it be true that the heart, by becoming familiar with scenes of suffering and violence, becomes obdurate at the sight; forgets its best quality, compassion; and feels less reluctance at inflicting pain when under the influence of irascible affections; and that this is true, none will deny, who know the force of habit, and the proneness of the mind to evil.

I believe that those who endeavour to find political reasons to justify the prevalence of a taste for boxing, are scarcely in earnest, and mean little more than to palliate with sophistry, what reason cannot approve. The taste arises among the lower orders, from natural brutality, or a wish to get money by entertaining their superiors in rank, who have disgracefully professed themselves *amateurs* of the practice. In the higher ranks, it arises from thoughtlessness, wantonness, and a gross ignorance of better modes of spending time, filling the chasms of science, polite arts, and philosophy.

But whatever it originates in, I shall not hesitate to assert, that it is unworthy of a gentleman, unworthy of a good citizen, unworthy of a Christian, and unworthy of a man.

I have said little of it in a religious view; though much might be said, for Christianity must condemn it entirely, without reserve, and without exception. But it is to be feared, that the fraternity of boxers and their followers will not lend a willing ear to the still small voice of religious conscience. Indeed I do not flatter myself with the idea of making converts of them by any thing which can be addressed to them in writing; for it is extremely probable, that those who are sunk so deeply in degeneracy, as to delight in this irrational and disgraceful amusement, take no delight in reading any thing but a sporting calendar, a book of farriery, or a treatise on the *science*, as they call, by way of eminence, the theory and sublime art of bruising the flesh, breaking the bones, and *sewing* up the eyes of their fellow-creatures.

But there is one great teacher who will be heard;

and whose arrival may probably be accelerated by reducing the *science*, which they admire, to practice. His instructions will cause them to see their conduct in a new light, and to despise their choice of spending the short space of life allotted to man in a behaviour more brutal than that of the beasts who perish, but who never exhibit the bloody effects of rage, except when they are impelled by real passion, in defence of their young, or the necessities of hunger.

======

NUMBER XXX.

On associating with Equals for the true Pleasure of Friendship.—Ev. 30.

THE experience of the world has long pronounced those marriages the happiest, in which the contracting parties are of a condition nearly equal; so that, when the first ardours of love are abated by time, neither can assume a superiority, or think it a condescension, to have acceded to the nuptial alliance.

This observation, which is just in matrimony, is no less true in friendship; of which, similar inclinations and similar aversions are said to constitute the only firm foundation. But to like and dislike the same or similar things, is not usual in persons widely separated from each other by birth, rank, and fortune. A great disparity in all these circumstances, causes things to appear in different colours, opens diversified prospects in life, and renders the same objects, to one desirable, and to the other, indifferent or odious.

Wherever, therefore, what the world, in common

language, terms friendships, are made between inferiors and superiors, plebeians and patricians, the connexion is not properly what the ancients understood by friendship, but a coalition formed by solicitation on one side, and condescension on the other, between an expecting dependant, and a powerful patron.   An alliance of this kind, though not abounding in the pleasures of true friendship, may be very useful to both parties; it may serve the necessities or convenience of the superior, and contribute to the interest, preferment, indulgence, and luxury, of the inferior; and is therefore very ardently and consistently pursued by those to whom these are the sole or principal objects in the establishment of an amicable intercourse.

But there are some who pursue such connexions exclusively of all others; and not so much for the sake of advancing their interest, as gratifying their pride and vanity. They scorn to admit their equals in birth, rank, fortune, and education, to that familiarity which true friendship requires. They hunt for men adorned with titles, or furnished with property, not in the least regarding the recommendation of personal worth. When admitted to the tables and company of such men, they become flatterers and humble servants, but cannot be considered as friends, in the just and honourable sense of that appellation. They are not in a state of liberty. They dare not express their real sentiments, lest they should give offence, and be excluded from the table, to sit at which, they consider as their chief good, their highest honour. If they possess the privilege of being allowed to leave a card at a great man's door, or can say among those whom they consider as their inferiors, that, the other day, they dined with their friend, Lord Slender, and must absolutely sup to-night with Lady Rout, where they expect to shake hands with an old friend, whom they have not seen some time, the Duke of Dolittle; they are supremely happy; they have not lived in vain; heaven has at last rewarded them amply for the pains they took in studying the *open countenance*, and *thoughts close;* the graces of the person, and the various modes of simulation and dissimulation.

After all, this lord, lady, and duke, only laugh at the poor fellow's folly, admitting him now and then to fill a chair, because he plays cards pretty well, sings a good song, blows the German flute, talks nonsense fluently, or romps with the children.

He, poor mortal! thinks his fortune made. No place becomes vacant, but he imagines his great friends may procure it for him. He knows they mean to do him some service by surprise, while they scarcely ever think about him, and would not give six-pence to save him from a prison. As to the little power they possess in procuring places, it has been all engaged for years to come, in securing the interest of two or three boroughs; and their good friend, who is so proud of their friendship, stands no more chance of preferment from them, than the pious and learned curate of their parishes, with forty pounds a year, and a wife and ten children.

What advantage, then, has he derived from his splendid connexions? Good dinners, good wine, sometimes good company, much amusement, and some improvement in the airs and manners of a man of fashion. What have these advantages cost him? The loss of the real pleasure and benefits he would have derived from his own family connexions, from several of his school-fellows, and his neighbours; every one of whom he has affronted, or deserted, since he first aspired at friendship with people in high life. He meets them either with a supercilious air, and a strut of self-consequence, or with that prodigious affability, and outrageous condescension, which proud people often display while they affect humility; and with which they insult and hurt, while they compliment and caress their dependant. His old friends, thus despised, retaliate upon him richly, and have long stigmatized the would-be-great man, with the mock-title of a Count.

Pleasure he may have enjoyed from such connexions; pleasure arising from the gratification of pride and vanity; but not the pleasure of cordial friendship. This is only to be found among persons whose condition in life is nearly equal; I say nearly equal, for a mathematical equality can never be found between any two persons, neither is it required for the establishment and enjoyment of friendship. A very considerable latitude must always be allowed to the word *equals*, when applied to friends; but not that latitude, which separates them at so great a distance, as renders condescension on one part, and submission on the other, necessary to form the unnatural coalition. In the physical attraction of cohesion, two drops containing a quantity of matter nearly equal, will mutually move towards each other; but if one drop is much larger, it will absorb the smaller, and appropriate it entirely. Wood of any kind may be joined to wood, by the common cement of the mechanic; but wood will not coalesce with gold and diamonds, without particular contrivance; and a slight accident will usually dissever the union.

The genuine pleasures of conversation are much diminished by restraint, awe, obsequiousness, and a fear of hurting one's interest in maintaining the free sentiments of conviction. Reason feels itself, in such circumstances, confined by trammels, which while they confine the motions, gall by their pressure. Freedom is lost; and it is an old observation, that slavery contributes to degeneracy of nature, as well as to misery. And I think it probable, that voluntary slavery is more degrading than compelled, since it argues a natural propensity to that meanness, which coercion is said in time to produce.

But, notwithstanding all that may be said, there are persons who make it the first objects of their lives to seek the friendship of persons greatly their superiors; and who avoid familiarity with their equals with as much solicitude as they would shun a pestilence. They cultivate the external graces, which in them are unbecoming; they engage in expensive pursuits, which their fortunes cannot support; they waste their time, which might be spent in honourable and lucrative employments, solely that they may dangle after persons in high life, who often despise their meanness, while, for their own accommodation or amusement, they admit their visits, and accept their attentions. Many a one has spent his life in pursuit of glittering phantoms, and lived to repent, in old age, poverty, and desertion, that he did not cultivate those friends, whom Providence had pointed out for his choice, by their proximity of situation, and similitude of manners, rank, and objects in life. Had he chosen his friends in his own sphere, he might have lived in a state of competency, and with respect; but as he chose to soar above them, with wings too feeble to support his flight, he fell unpitied by those whom he deserted, and contemned by those whom he vainly attempted to reach. A toad eater, a led captain, an humble companion, are appellations which no man, who has a sense of real honour, would choose to possess; but these are the best names bestowed upon men who spend their lives in courting the great by all arts, but those of truth and virtue.

Every man should respect himself as a man. The conscious dignity which, in the lowest station, preserves the mind from unmanly meanness, is not the pride against which philosophy protests, and Christian meekness revolts. All respect, indeed, should be paid to superiors in civil rank, which the love of order dictates, which local customs or national institutions require; which decorum, and even fashion, when she is not exorbitant, may direct; but no man who has a just idea of what it is to be a man, will sacrifice his liberty, his freedom of thinking and speaking, all the frank joys of social intercourse, to a fellow-creature exalted above him, not by personal worth, but by adventitious and hereditary honour; and one who probably never intends to reward the sacrifice, by any thing but a nod and a smile. For such a sacrifice, indeed, no man, however elevated, can make an adequate remuneration.

There is certainly no reason to avoid, but many to seek, the notice and patronage of the *worthy great*, by worthy conduct; but if the aspirant is a gentleman, by which I mean a man of real honour, duly accomplished by education, he must be admitted to their friendship on terms of perfect equality, as a gentleman; and the distinction of the nobleman must be absorbed in the cordiality of the friend. Otherwise the connexion, however glossed by specious names, is like that of the old feudal times, between the lord and his vassal.

What has been said on the necessity of a nearly equal condition, to the existence of true friendship, must be extended to connexions with those too much below, as well as those too much above us. But pride is usually a sufficient guard against excessive condescension, in the selection of cordial friends; and it is, indeed, experimentally certain, that low connexions are usually the destruction of all the improvements of education, and the refined polish of higher life. But let it be remembered, that when *low* is synonymous with *vulgar*, there are many persons very low, who yet are high in rank, and affluent in fortune.

It seems to be no improper conclusion, that, if preferment and promotion are our objects in forming connexions, we ought to seek them rationally and by worthy conduct, from superiors; if the enjoyment of social delight and hearty friendship, from our equals; if opportunities of doing good most effectually, from our inferiors; but that no object whatever in forming connexions, can justify the sacrifice of freedom, reason, and conscience, which constitute the true dignity of human nature.

NUMBER XXXI.

On the beneficial Effects of the Marine Society.
Ev. 31.

'SIR,

'You desired me to write down the few particulars of my life, that you might be able to communicate them to a member of the Marine Society. I comply with your request most readily; but, at the same time, must entreat you to put my narrative into better language than I am able to use, since I never was scholar enough to indite a letter fit for the inspection of any body but one of my shipmates.

'My parents, during the winter, lived in a garret in Kent-street, and followed the employment of raking kennels, picking up rags and bones, and sifting cinders in a neighbouring brickfield. In the summer, they took a journey into Kent, and procured a precarious livelihood by hay-making, harvest work of all kinds, and picking of hops. They journeyed in a de-

cent style, for folks in their condition, having an ass,
a pair of panniers, and a tin kettle.

'The first event of any great importance to me, which
I can remember, was a violent dispute between my
father and mother, while they were making tea under a hedge, by the side of the Kent-road. My mother, it seems, usually kept the money, and as the hop-
picking was just ended, the store was pretty plentiful.   My father insisted in taking out of the leathern
purse enough to supply him with a dram of gin after
tea.   My mother peremptorily refused, as she had
formed a design of buying me a pair of breeches as
soon as we should reach London.   Words were high.
My father swore terribly; and after obtaining the
purse, by intimidating my mother with an uplifted
hedge stake, walked away, solemnly vowing that he
would go on ship-board, and never see us more. My
mother, putting the panniers on the ass, and me into
one of them, set off in immediate pursuit: but my father, as we supposed, turned out of the road, and we
were never able to find him. We pursued our journey,
and arrived at our old quarters in Kent-street at midnight. It was too late to be admitted; and we remain-
ed cold and hungry in the street all night.   In the
morning we expected admission to our lodgings; but
the pay being exacted previously to entrance, and it
being discovered that we had lost all our money, the
ass, panniers, and kettle, were seized for an old debt,
and we ourselves turned from the door to seek our
fortune.

'Beggary was now our only resource. As I had neither shirt, breeches, stockings, nor shoes, and indeed
no covering whatever but an old ragged petticoat of
my mother's, thrown over my shoulders, I moved the
compassion of many passengers, and earned, upon the
average, four-pence a day. This served to keep us
from starving, but could not furnish us with a lodging

at night. But there are comforts in all situations. The neighbouring brickhill furnished us with a warm lodging, at no expense. Hither we used to retire, as soon as it was dark, and often slept more soundly than the rich on their beds of down. One morning, however, to my great grief and surprise, I found my mother dead by my side. She had drunk a little too much gin on the preceding evening, and her health being impaired by grief and want, she fell asleep to wake no more. I knew not what to do. Hunger impelled me to return to the street and beg. I sallied forth, with an intention to return again in the evening, and see whether any care had been taken of the corpse; but as I was rambling about, I met a boy of similar appearance with myself, and we soon entered into familiar conversation. I told him my wants. He could not relieve them, for his own distresses were equally great; but he undertook to conduct me to the quays, near the custom-house, where, he said, I might live most luxuriously on sugar, by watching my opportunities to pick and scrape the hogsheads, as soon as they were landed. I listened with delight; and we ran with eagerness to the place where he said he had lived pleasantly for some months. I found his representation true. Sugar, treacle, and raisins, were our delicious viands. They were often mixed with dirt, for we chiefly picked them from the ground; but hunger is not nice: and though they were filthy, they were sweet. The only misfortune was, that we seldom could procure enough to satisfy the demands of nature; and we were nearly starved to death in the midst of our luscious repasts.

' One day, as I was busy in scraping the inside of an empty hogshead, I was accosted by a fat, ruddy, old woman, decently dressed, in the following words: " Child," said she, " you seem to be of an active disposition. You might earn a better livelihood than this,

if you were inclined to be industrious. If you will
come along with me, I will clothe you, and set you
up in a business that may make your fortune; and as
an earnest of my favour, take this roll and cheese.'
I seized the food, with the voraciousness of a hungry
lion, and devoured it before I made the least reply.
She repeated her question, whether I was willing to
go home with her? I scarcely answered for joy; but
leaping out of the hogshead, with the utmost agility,
placed myself at due distance behind her, to follow
wherever she might please to lead. She walked on
through various turnings and windings, till she came
to a little house in a blind alley, which I have since
learned is called Cut-throat Corner.

'As soon as I had eaten and drunk sufficiently, she
caused me to be washed perfectly clean, and my hair
to be cut off almost as close as if I had been shaved.
She then clothed me from head to foot, in old and
dirty garments, but tolerably tight and warm. You
may easily suppose that I was delighted with this
change of fortune. I was put to bed on a flock bed,
which appeared to me most delicately soft; but I
could not sleep for thinking of the happiness I enjoyed.

'The next morning, my patroness told me that she
had chosen me from many others whom she had seen
on the quays; because she had observed my great
activity, and particularly admired the nimbleness of
my fingers; that she thought me perfectly well qualified, by nature and genius, for the employment she
intended me, and that a few lessons would complete
me in the practice; that my business was to ease
careless gentlemen and ladies, in crowds, of their
watches and pocket-handkerchiefs; and that I must
begin with the pocket-handkerchief department.
Upon this, she shewed me her pocket, and made me
take out her handkerchief a hundred times, till I could

do it with a kind of legerdemain, without her perceiving it. I was no unapt scholar; and on the first day of my noviciate, arrived at a considerable degree of dexterity.

"Well," said she, "I will accompany you this evening to the play-house door, and continue in the neighbourhood till the time of business is expected. If you bring home one handkerchief, I shall continue you in my service ; but remember, if you have no success; I will cause you to be taken up as a pickpocket, and sent to prison. Go*," said she, "and prosper. Improve in your new art; thus may you arrive at riches. Remember that all depends upon your merit."

' I arrived at the scene of action, and, with great fear and trembling, began to think of reducing my theory to practice. Often I attempted to *dive*, and as often withdrew my trembling fingers. At last I saw an elderly gentleman, very handsomely dressed in a bag-wig, his hat under one arm, and an umbrella in the other hand. Now, said I, is the time. Now must I succeed in bearing off the prize, or a prison, and poverty, and hunger, will be my lot. This thought urged me to attempt. I plunged my hand into his pocket. I pulled the handkerchief, but it was pinned to the bottom. The sudden jerk roused the gentleman's attention. He seized me by the collar, and dragged me, without making any disturbance, into a quiet street in the neighbourhood.

"My lad," said he, "I see you are very young, and your countenance, as far as I can judge by this light, looks ingenuous and honest. I pity you. Perhaps you may have found a friend in me. Tell me by what circumstances you were led to this life of villany?"

' I fell down upon my knees, implored his pardon,

---

* I, pede fausto———

    Macte novà virtute, puer.—VIRG.

and told him, in as few words as possible, the heads of my history.

'Upon my finishing it, I thought I saw him wipe a drop from his eyes with his white handkerchief; but he turned aside lest I should discover it.

'Assuming a stern manner, which I could see was the effect of his judgment acting against his nature, he told me, that though my crime deserved the severe punishment of the law, yet he would endeavour to reform, rather than torment me, if I were good enough, and sensible enough, to suffer him to snatch me from destruction.

'He added, "As you have no friends, or parents, to distress by your absence, you shall go home with me to-night; and to-morrow, I will take such measures with you as I shall see proper." So saying, he called a coach, and making me enter it with him, he ordered it to drive to his house.

'Not to tire you with an enumeration of particulars, he recommended me as an object of charity to the Marine Society; and while he related my misfortunes, kindly concealed my crime.

'I was cleansed, clothed, instructed, and sent to sea. I enjoyed a happiness which no language can describe, in obtaining the means of earning an honest livelihood. I felt a sentiment of religious gratitude to the author of my being, and the preserver of my life. I wished to read the Scriptures, and was fortunate to find a shipmate who bestowed great pains upon me, in a long voyage, and taught me, eager as I was to learn, both to read and write. My regularity and diligence gained the esteem of the officers; and whatever favour could be shewn me, without blamable partiality, I received. I had been early trained in the school of adversity, and was therefore the better prepared for the school of virtue. I distinguished myself in several engagements in the last war, and had the honour to lose my leg in the service. When the first pain and suffering was over, I felt great consolation in finding myself enriched by a pretty share of the prize-money. With this I took a good-accustomed shop in the chandlery line. It succeeded to my wish. I have been married some years to a most industrious woman. I have three boys, all of whom are sent to school, and can read and write well, though the eldest is not nine years old. I am respected by my neighbours; I am in a state of plenty; I am happy.

' And now, Sir, give me leave to request you to make my acknowledgments to the leading men of that admirable society, to which I am indebted for my rescue from all the wretchedness of extreme poverty, united with temptations to extreme wickedness; and for opportunities of becoming a useful member of the community, instead of a bane and a curse. O, Sir! none but those who have actually felt the beneficial effects of this institution, can conceive of them as they deserve. I have felt them; I therefore can form an adequate idea of them; but I want language for expression. Let me conclude my long epistle with a hope, that all who have the superfluities of life, will bestow some of them on the support of a society which patronises the outcasts of the human race, the naked, the hungry, the vagabond *infant* who cannot help himself, and has none to help him; too loathsome with filth, to be borne by delicacy; too obscure and concealed, to be seen by the eye of grandeur.'

Since my writing the above, I have heard of the REFORM in St. George's-fields. God prosper it. Pray present it with the enclosed *guinea*.

NUMBER XXXII.

_On the Influence of the Profession on the Manners and
the Character of the Professors._—Ev. 32.

THAT the daily actions and professional employments, in which men are conversant, produce an
effect on their manners, sentiments, and dispositions, is an opinion which none will be inclined to
controvert. Experience evinces that this effect is
sometimes beneficial, and sometimes injurious. The
immediate causes, and the nature of the influence
of _profession on character_, afford matter of curious
and important speculation.

In considering the subject, I shall take a view of
the profession of divinity, law, physic, and of the
military life. The subject is rather invidious; but
in pursuit of truth, the odium resulting from its discovery, must be borne with patience.

It is certain that no assertions can be made on
great numbers of men, which will continue to be
true of every individual. If they are true in general
the exceptions will not diminish their importance.

The clergy of England, considered as a body,
constitute a most respectable class; not to be excelled, in all that improves and reflects honour on
human nature, by any other body of the same number in the community. Liberally educated, attentive
to character, conversant in acts of Christian benevolence, employed in acquiring and communicating
knowledge of the most important kind, they shine
as lights in the world, diffusing, like the great lumi-
nary in nature, a radiance to guide, and a warmth to
foster the erring multitude. Their office, considered

speculatively, is most honourable and beneficent; and without flattery, it may be affirmed, that the clergy of England have acted up to it in practice, with a comparative uniformity of wisdom and virtue, which bears ample testimony to the truth of their religion, and refutes the infidel more effectually than all the folios of polemic disputation.

Thus they appear in their official or professional capacity. In familiar life, and the common intercourse of vicinity, they are social, pleasant, elegant, improving, and charitable. They cultivate every thing that can embellish and refine, together with all that can enlighten, soften, civilize, and purify the manners of society.

The important business of education has devolved upon them almost entirely, by the tacit consent even of the irreligious; a consent arising from conviction, that their morals and attainments usually render them the fittest persons to conduct it, with the greatest skill and fidelity. The princes and nobles of the land derive from their instructions, the wisdom and the eloquence necessary to govern nations; and the union of those brilliant and solid accomplishments, which add fresh lustre, and intrinsic weight, to crowns and coronets, stars and ribands. The lowest of the people find from the exertions of the clergy, an education suited to their humble sphere, leading to useful qualifications, inspiring religious principles, and all the humble virtues of industry. The clergy have confessedly handed down the torch of science from generation to generation, which, without their care, might have been long ago extinguished.

They are, indeed, philosophers dispersed over the nation; philosophers, but with all the pride of philosophy melted down by the charity and humility of the Christian; philosophers, but without the use-

less seclusion of mere contemplative life; philosophers, but such as bring down wisdom from heights
inaccessible to the vulgar, and cause her to walk
familiarly in the common road, among all the sons
of men, without any exclusive distinction of riches
and honours, loving and serving them all as children
of the same Parent, as inheritors of the same glory.

But is there no shade in the picture? Is there no
dross in the ore? I believe there is as little imper-
fection in the whole order, as the common infirmity
of human nature allows; but that little is usually
magnified by the tongues of those who, unfortunately
for themselves, endeavour to wound religion through
the sides of her ministers. It is easy to account for
the malignant representations of a Shaftesbury and
a Hume. The cause of their hatred of the clergy,
must destroy its effect on every mind, which unites
candour with good sense.

But it seems reasonable to suppose, that some less
laudable habits and dispositions may be caused by
a few untoward circumstances attending their profession. It certainly affords them much leisure;
and leisure is a temptation to indolence; and indolence is the parent of luxury, gluttony, and intemperance. It leads to a taste for trifles, to a love of
the various games of chance, of field sports, and
all the ingenious contrivances for killing time.
Happy, if it is confined to pastimes that are inoffensive, and negatively good; since the experience
of the world has long established, as an incontestable truth, that idleness is the root of all evil. It
cannot be expected, that all the individuals of a very
numerous class, should possess inclination and ability for the pursuits of literature. To such, the
mere business of supplying a church cannot afford
avocation enough to employ their time. As they
have no taste for study or composition, they have

recourse to the easy modes of supplying their pulpit, which modern contrivances amply furnish; and after expending a few pounds in this way, they have little to interrupt the studies of the card-table, and the amusements of the gun, the dog, the horse, and the bottle.

The love of money, as well as the love of pleasure, in excess, has been laid to their charge. Appearances may sometimes confirm the imputation. Their incomes are often small, and drop at once on their demise. A desire, therefore, to obtain independence in old age, or to provide for a family, leads to a parsimonious attention, which, by a hasty judgment, will be pronounced avarice. Their claims for tithes are made on those who, from their sordid dispositions, pay with reluctance, and are glad to resent a just demand, by stigmatizing him who makes it, with the epithet, covetous. The charge is often unjust; but yet it is easy to observe that frugality commonly degenerates, in old age, to downright and extreme avarice.

A mean submission to superiors, for the sake of emolument, is another characteristic which has been supposed to mark the profession. While men are actuated by the hope of gain, and the spur of ambition, they will take the most effectual methods of obtaining the object of their desire. And it happens unfortunately, that those who bestow preferment, are not so likely to bestow it on merit, of which they are often but incompetent judges; as on a submission to their will, and a subserviency to their purposes of pleasure, avarice, and ambition. The dog that fawns, it is remarked gets more bones and fragments from the master's table, than the surly mastiff who barks and growls, yet guards the house from the midnight depredator. Unmanly obsequiousness in this profession, may be easily ac-

R 2

counted for; but cannot be palliated in any other way, than by pleading the infirmity of human nature.

Much has been said on the *odium theologicum*, or the bitter hatred of divines, as if they were, above all men, implacable in their resentments. This aspersion might adhere to them in times of ignorance and barbarity; but in the present times, is totally inapplicable. The opinion arose from the unhappy virulence of controversialists. But among them also, the charge admits of extenuation or excuse. It was thrown upon them by their enemies; and if they gave any apparent occasion for it, which I fear must be acknowledged, let it be candidly believed, that their intemperate zeal arose from their earnestness and sincerity; honest qualities, and respectable even in a mistaken cause.

If these, or any other circumstances of the theological profession, lead to foibles or faults; to levities or vices; to pride or meanness; it will be right to guard with double vigilance against an assault in the weakest place. ' Let not your good be evil spoken of,' is a scriptural caution. It is peculiarly necessary to avoid this evil in the church; because not only the individuals who are censured, suffer, but the church itself, and those over whom they are appointed to watch as shepherds; and before whom they are to walk as exemplary guides. Methodists and infidels are equally extreme to mark what is done amiss by that order which is countenanced and protected by church and state. Their severity is unchristian and irrational: but, such is the malignity of mankind, that it is found to serve their cause, by making proselytes to their opinions. And I fear, it is not a false alarm, nor a needless admonition, to say, that both these descriptions of men have increased, are increasing, and ought to be diminished. But how diminished? Not by persecution, but by the mild, yet irresistible compulsion of sound argument, enforced by a brilliant example of Christian perfection, I must retract the word *perfection*. None of us can reach it; and woe to them who judge others, whether believers or unbelievers, clergy or laity, methodists or atheists, with excessive rigour. All men are servants of one Master, by whose judgment they shall stand or fall. Let each judge himself with severity; but all others, with that lenity, which himself must most devoutly wish for, at the tribunal of the righteous Judge.

NUMBER XXXIII.

On the Influence of the Medical Profession on the Manners.—Ev. 33.

If great respect is paid to speculative science, to pure mathematics, to astronomy, to metaphysics, to all the effects of ingenuity which terminate in the sublime and refined pleasure of intellectual exercise; how much more justly is it due to a science which prepares itself by speculation, merely that it may descend to practice; that it may learn to assuage the agony of pain, resuscitate the languor of sickness, preserve or restore the impaired senses, render old age easy, and lengthen life? A speculative philosopher, however excellent, even a Newton and a Locke, weighed in the scales of reason, against a practising physician of skill and virtues like those of a Heberden, or a Willis, kick the beam like the gossamer that floats in the air, balanced with a wedge of bullion.

As life abounds with misery, they are to be con-

R 3

sidered as the greatest men, and the most honourable members of society, who are best able to relieve it. What avails it to miserable man *(œgris mortalibus,* as Virgil feelingly expresses it) that a new planet is discovered; or a new moon belonging to an old planet; or the doctrine of innate ideas; or liberty and necessity, confirmed or invalidated? But it concerns him beyond expression, when a remedy is pointed out for the gout, the stone, a fever; for blindness, deafness, lameness, madness; for the preservation of his life, or the lives of those, in whom his whole happiness is involved.

The profession of a physician is, therefore, worthy of high honour, and will receive it from those who form a just idea of real utility, and bestow their esteem, not on the dazzling objects of empty pretension, but on that which confers the most substantial and unequivocal benefit on the human race.

Thus noble is the profession of medicine; and the professors of it in England, have usually acted up to its dignity. Deeply learned in philosophy; well versed in polite letters; adorned with arts; graced with social accomplishments; and, above all, tinctured with humanity; they have charmed in the common intercourse of conversation, and approached the sick bed with the appearance of guardian angels.

The common-place wit on the inutility of the science, and the vanity and venality of its professors, will be little regarded by him who has felt its benign operation on himself, or seen it displayed with the skill and compassion of a superior Being, on those whom he loved; in the hour of unspeakable tribulation, when hope, the last friend of the distressed, began to spread her wings, and prepare for departure: who has also seen the preserver of a family's peace, in his social evening, diffusing the brilliancy of wit, and the radiance of knowledge, with a gay cheerfulness of heart and countenance, arising from the consciousness of having spent the day in alleviating woe.

Who but must lament that any circumstances in such a profession, should lead to a behaviour exposed to satire or ridicule? But *they say* (to use a favourite, though rather a detracting phrase of an ingenious prelate), *they say*, that physicians are pompous, self-sufficient, affectedly solemn, venal, and unfeeling.

The great respect which is usually and very properly paid to their directions, by the anxious persons, who solicit their assistance, may, perhaps, accustom them to consider themselves entitled to a kind of despotism. Of the physician, it may be said, *he rules o'er willing slaves*[*], and his air of self-sufficiency and pomp, though exposed to the witticism of the comic muse, may produce at the bedside of the invalid, a beneficial effect. Confidence raises in the patient and the by-standers a high opinion of the doctor; especially among the lower ranks of people. They have observed but little, who have not remarked, how much imagination contributes to give success to the curative power of a medicine. If the pomp and self-sufficiency thus adopted, in the exercise of the art, are likely to extend themselves to common life, they are in danger of just derision; and therefore, a sensible physician will be on his guard, lest a behaviour, which on some occasions, may be proper and useful, should, by becoming habitual, and appearing at improper times, sully a character which has a right to shine with undiminished lustre.

The appearance of mystery, which is often blamed, is not without good effects on patients, who, from a natural propensity of human nature, are apt to venerate, and confide in most, what they least understand. Many, if they were fully to comprehend the

* Per populos dat jura volentes.—VIRG.

nature of the remedies administered, would despise,
and refuse to apply them. The satire and ridicule
so liberally, or rather illiberally, thrown on the physician for these appearances, in the exercise of his
profession, is unjust; and ought then only to be applied to him, when he assumes them in the scenes of
domestic and social life.

That physicians are peculiarly venal, is, I believe,
false. Few can be named who do not give much of
their time and skill to the afflicted poor, to their own
professions, and to the clergy, without accepting the
smallest recompense. Many have been known to
return great part of exorbitant fees, given by the
grateful rich, endeavouring to proportion their own
remuneration to the good they may have been able
to do, and the attendance they have been obliged to
give. But the assumption of a profession will not
alter a radical disposition of the heart. Some among
the medical class, as well as in all other classes, are
naturally covetous; and the meanness and harpy
avarice of a few has unjustly been suffered to fix a
mark of disgrace on all. The common fee of a physician, considering the expense of his education, and
that he sells no medicine, is moderate; nor can he
be blamed, who accepts, under the guidance of discretion and humanity, the recompense of an employment by which himself, and perhaps a family, are to
be supported.

That medical men are unfeeling, is an opinion,
which arises from their coolness and dispassionate
deportment in the midst of deep distress. But this
command of their feelings is a prime excellence in
their character. While all around them are embarrassed and debilitated by sorrow, they are called upon
to act with wisdom and judgment. Were they to
sink under sympathy, the patient whom they came
to relieve, must be neglected, or attended to with

faculties deranged, confused, and unable to prescribe
with decision.

But still it must be allowed, that an habitual sight
of distress diminishes sensibility. Physicians, therefore, who act with humanity, as the greater part certainly do, are the more to be esteemed, since they
counteract the effect of their familiarity with scenes
of suffering, by the control of their reason. If, without feeling, they act with all the kind attention which
feeling would cause, combined with the steadiness of
cool judgment, which excessive feeling might shake,
they are entitled to the praise, which mere animal or
instinctive sensibility can never deserve.

I do not find any peculiar failing originating from
the circumstances of the profession, in the character
of the physician; and those which are alleged by
prejudice and vulgarity, are either nonentities, or
such infirmities as fall to the lot of all men. If there
is any thing singular in this profession, it is singular
ingenuity, singular politeness, and singular beneficence. As to the empirical tribe, the disgrace of
society; the reverse of every thing said in praise of
the physician, will, in general, be applicable to them;
and it must be the wish of all benevolent men, that
the deceptions which they obtrude on afflicted poverty and ignorance, were by authority of law cog-
nizable by a court of sworn physicians, and punish-
able by a severe penalty. There are few greater
abuses in a community, than that of picking the
pockets of those who are already distressed by penury and disease united; and preventing them from
applying where relief might be obtained, by holding
out specious pretensions corroborated by false and
venal testimonies. The ridicule and censure which
have been unjustly thrown on the physicians, are
justly due to the quack-doctors. They are, indeed,
pompous, self-sufficient, affectedly solemn, venal,

and unfeeling with a vengeance. If there were a tribunal, at which the assumption of doctor's degrees could be investigated, it might be serviceable in detecting and exposing one mode of deceit, by which ignorant empirics impose on vulgar credulity.

Surgeons and apothecaries regularly trained and improved by experience, may certainly take a rank next to the physician. Their skill and humanity in the present age entitle them to a more honourable place in society, than they have formerly been allowed. Men of sense are not guided in their judgment by an appellation. Surgeons and apothecaries enjoying and using the opportunities for improvement, which, in these times, are afforded more plentifully than ever, become, in effect, and in the liberal sense of the term, physicians. From their extensive researches, and from their general intercourse in families, their minds are as enlightened, and their conversation as polite and agreeable, as those of any order in the community.

I cannot dismiss this part of my subject without doing justice to the university of Edinburgh, by acknowledging that much of that superior excellence which distinguishes the medical classes in all their branches, throughout Great Britain, is derived from the instruction it affords. Edinburgh, as a place of medical education, has confessedly surpassed, not only Oxford and Cambridge, but the universities of all Europe.

NUMBER XXXIV.

On the influence of the profession of the Law on the Manners.— Ev. 34.

LAW, the accumulated wisdom of ages, forms a stately and massy pile, which it is impossible to contemplate without feeling a reverential respect, resembling, in some degree, religious adoration. The aggregated decisions of the wisest and best of men, augmented, retrenched, corrected by the cautious hand of experience, and at last confirmed and compacted by the slow but powerful operation of time, demand an admiration of their excellence, and an acquiescence in their wisdom, almost equal to the implicit submission paid to revelations from ON HIGH.

Those men, therefore, in society, whose office it is to preserve the law, to expound it, and to administer it, deserve, if they execute their office well, to wear the robe of distinction, and to be seated at the right hand of the prince. While they poise the scales of equity, and wield the sword of justice, let them be crowned with the wreath of civic honour.

But a truce with the flights of imaginary perfection. Law, however pure and excellent in itself, is but a dead letter, till it is called into life by the activity of man; of man, weak in his nature, corrupt in his will, and prone to pervert the best things for the narrow purposes of selfish advantage.

Law constitutes a venal profession, in which the sublime views of equity are often obscured and lost, in the misty mazes of chicane. Cunning, as often as wisdom, assumes the office of interpretation, and, by successful subtilty, rises to high honours among men, wears the trappings, and enjoys the recompense of that wisdom which she has ingeniously aped, though she could not equal.

The great lawyers, who have reached the highest honours of appointment and nobility, began their career as advocates at the tribunal. As advocates, their study was not so much to point out the law as it really existed, as to sophisticate the letter, and misrepresent the spirit of it, in order to serve the temporary purpose of the client who paid the fee. As hired advocates, they were obliged in honour (a sort of honour which binds even highwaymen) to defend, with all their knowledge and eloquence, the cause they undertook, whether right or wrong; and thus a plausible sophistry was often of higher value, and more ardently studied, than truth, reason, law, or equity. To gain the cause was the object; not to illustrate law; not to do justice between man and man; but to gain the cause;—which was, in effect, to gain popularity, employments, riches, office, and perhaps, at last, titular distinction.

But minds thus habituated to sophistry, are in danger of suffering cunning to become their predominant quality, conspicuous in every part of life. Having found it successful in their profession, they infer its efficacy in the commerce of society, in common intercourse, and in familiar conversation. But cunning, it has long been observed, is not compatible with greatness of mind, or comprehensive wisdom; and it is remarkable, that the most successful advocates at the bar, have not usually been the best ministers of state, members of parliament, magistrates, patriots, or men.

Great cunning is, indeed, scarcely compatible with strict honesty. It tempts to the violation of it by pointing out the means and by suggesting the chances of impunity. Characters, therefore, in the

law, which have been admired for ability, have often
been viewed with suspicion, on the points of integrity
and principle. The appearances of them have been
supposed by the world to be adopted from the same
cunning which has regulated every part of their conduct, and laid the foundation of riches and honours.
Few famous advocates and practising lawyers, therefore, considering the great numbers in the profession, are ranked among the great benefactors of
mankind. After their death, and when the interested individuals, who have been served by their
cunning, have been silenced by the universal Level-
ler, they have been considered as little more than
*artful fabricators of their own fortune**. No idea has
been attached to them, in the least resembling such
as are affixed to the character of the Solons, the
Lycurgi, the Numæ, and the Minos's of antiquity.

It is, indeed, a standing proof of the little intrinsic
value of human honours, that they have been lavished, with a peculiar profusion, on a profession
singularly selfish, and singularly disposed to injure
the great interests of society, for the advantage of
particulars. But its success in the world is easily
accounted for. It makes cordial friends, by serving
secular purposes; by securing victory in doubtful
rivalries; by assisting men in things which they are
apt to deem paramount to all, in the great contests
for riches, power, and honour. The glorious un-
certainty of the law renders it, in the hands of a
skilful practitioner, an instrument to his avarice and
ambition, in being made to bend, like a leaden rule,
to the wishes and views of every bountiful employer.

But if the profession of the law has this corrupt-
ing influence on the minds of the advocates, men
usually improved by a liberal education, and elevated by nobler views, how baneful must be its ope-

* Fabre quisque fartunæ suæ—Cɪᴄ.

ration on the lower practitioners! how much more
so on the pettyfoggers; men, low in rank, low in
principle, and low in education! But here I will
observe a tender silence. I am unwilling to inflame
that odium, which, confounding the innocent with
the guilty, has branded the whole tribe with charges
of duplicity, management, artifice, and trickishness,
approaching to the imputation of arrant knavery. I
mean not to satirize, but to admonish. If there are
peculiar circumstances in the lower parts of the
profession, which tempt to a disingenuous, over-
reaching, crooked conduct, let the professors be
doubly guarded against them, as men, in the first
place; and in the second, as men in a profession.
It is certain, that a fair character, exclusively of all
ideas of the loveliness and virtue of rectitude, is the
most conducive to success in the business of an
attorney. And let no prospect of present gain tempt
a man to hazard an imputation on his character; a
loss, which the gain of dishonest practice can never
compensate.

The letter of the law allows many things which
are extremely hard, if not strictly unjust. Those
who are obliged to act by the letter of the law, unfortunately incur a blame in such cases, which is
certainly not their due. But a man of sense and
humanity, who values his character and conscience,
will avoid, as much as possible, such practice as
leads to the doing what is rigid, under the sanction
of what is lawful. The levying of distress, and all
kinds of petty litigation, afford very dangerous temptations to the commission of cruelty, the suppression
of truth, the propagation of scandal, and the support
of plausible falsehood. Men whose natural dispositions and acquired principles reprobate such things,
are sometimes ensnared into them by the untoward
circumstances of their professional employment. The

world should make some allowances for a conduct, which, though far from laudable, is rendered, by the entanglements of a difficult and dangerous business, not easy to be avoided.

Unnecessary reserve and caution are observed to mark the conversation of many in this profession; a reserve and caution acquired by attending to the force of words in legal instruments, and the various meanings that are often given to little or no meaning in courts of judicature. But these frigid qualities cast a damp on the ardour of cordial familiarity, give an alarm of design, and either shut up the mouths of the company, or render the discourse stiff, formal, and insincere, from a superfluity of circumspection.

A disposition to wrangle, contradict, and controvert opinions on trifling subjects; to argue, not on points of real consequence, but about a pin's point; a *captiousness*, a *dictatorial air*, a *supercilious insolence*, and a *perpetual attempt at wit*, derived from *imitating eminent counsellors at the bar*, often spoil the conversation of men who, from their evident talents in the practice of the law, might be expected to furnish improving topics of friendly discourse. But these are foibles little to be regarded in men, who preserve their characters in weightier matters, free from just reproach.

And notwithstanding the dangers peculiar to the business of an advocate, and the practice of an attorney, there are, doubtless many who overcome them all; who walk through the mazes of a wilderness, without deviating into crooked paths, without wounding themselves with the brambles, or defiling themselves with the mire.

NUMBER XXXV.

On the Influence of the Military Profession on the Manners, with a General Conclusion on the Subject.— Ev. 35.

NOTWITHSTANDING the historian records, with all the dignity of language, the achievements of the warrior; the orator celebrates him in the most splendid panegyric; the poet adds new brilliancy to his character, by the colours of fancy, and the graces of diction; yet that state of war which gives opportunities for all this display of glory, cannot but appear, in the eyes of philosophy and religion, not only the calamity, but the disgrace of human nature. Neither the purposes of regal ambition, nor the pretences of political interest and national aggrandizement, nothing but inevitable necessity and self-defence, can justify a state of war; that state which spreads misery and desolation, and instigates poor short-sighted and short-lived fellow-creatures to cut off each other, as far as they are able, from the face of the earth, on which God placed them to be happy.

But in vain do reason and philosophy lift up their voices amidst the tumultuous din of disordered passions. War always subsisted on some part of the globe, and will probably continue, while false politics and corrupt and malignant passions predominate, and while the vices of men require a scourge.

Men in the military profession are not culpable for the existence of a state which they found established before they were born, and which it is not in their power, if it were their inclination, to alter. Their profession has always been deemed one of the

most honourable. As things are constituted, and
as they have generally conducted themselves, their
claim to honour may, I believe, remain undisputed.
While we lament that such an order of men should
have been found necessary, we may freely bestow
that praise which the virtues of individuals engaged
in it deserve.

Courage is, obviously, a prime requisite in this
profession. It has, of course, been cultivated, encouraged, and displayed by it in high perfection.
But courage, when it does not arise from animal insensibility, is connected with every generous virtue.
The soldier has therefore been distinguished for
openness, honour, truth, and liberality. To the
solid virtues, he has also added the high polish of
urbane and easy manners. His various commerce
with the living world has rubbed off those asperities,
and extended that narrowness, which too often adhere to the virtuous recluse. And perhaps it is difficult to exhibit human nature in a more amiable and
honourable light, than it appears in the accomplished
soldier; in the soldier, fully prepared for his profession by a liberal education, and finished, through
the favourable circumstances of it, by all those qualities which render men generous in principle, and
agreeable in conversation.

But all the professions are found to have some
circumstances unfavourable, as well as favourable, to
rectitude and propriety; some peculiar temptations
which lead imperceptibly, without uncommon caution, to error, absurdity, and vice. I endeavour to
point them out, not with a desire to disgrace, but to
add new honours to the profession, and to render
what sullies them more conspicuous, that it may be
more easily avoided. He who fixes a buoy over a
rock or a quicksand, does not intimate by it, that
navigation is not to be followed or encouraged; but

by pointing out local and partial danger, facilitates and secures the increase and success of navigation.

The profession of a soldier naturally leads to the cultivation of bodily strength, agility, and grace. But a great attention to the body, especially at an early age, may preclude that attention to the mind which is necessary to solid improvement. There is therefore danger, lest only a superficial knowledge of letters, or even ignorance of a very disgraceful kind, should be a characteristic of a great number in the profession. But ignorance must always lower the character of a gentleman. It may also lead to a variety of follies, scarcely to be avoided by him who, possessing a great deal of leisure, knows not how to employ it in the amusements of a library, or in the conversation of intelligent society.

But exclusively of the general knowledge, which, in the present age, is necessary to all who support with consistency the character of a gentleman, there is a great deal of professional science required to form the accomplished soldier. Many parts of mathematics, tactics, fortification, geography, and modern history, those parts more particularly which describe battles and sieges, are no less necessary to make an officer, than his commission.

The lives of great generals are well worth the attention of those who mean to arrive at a distinguished height in military excellence. The writers on the art military (*scriptores de re militari*), both ancient and modern, will also claim a considerable share of his application.

The art of drawing must be singularly useful to the soldier ; forming, if he has any natural turn to it, a most pleasing amusement, and a very valuable qualification for the exercise of his profession.

The soldier who neglects all these, to attend solely to external grace and bodily exercise, must have a mind empty of every solid attainment, and open to the admission of vanity and vice. And there is great danger lest he should neglect them, arising from the uncommon temptations to gaiety and dissipation which surround his profession. Acceptable to all companies, caressed by the gay, and admired by the fair, he finds it difficult to withdraw his attention from the lively scene before him, to devote it to study and contemplation. He is in peculiar danger of falling into licentiousness and libertinism. Experience has confirmed what speculation has suggested. All the dissolute manners of idleness, habits of excessive drinking, and debauchery; habits of gaming, swearing, expense, and contracting debt, have too often disgraced a profession, which men have ever been inclined to treat with honour; and rendered a mode of life, which is at best exposed to many evils and inconveniences, infinitely more uncomfortable, by pecuniary distress and bodily disease.

The naval officer must be comprehended under the military profession. The sun in his whole progress through the heavens does not behold a class of men more uniformly generous, manly, and brave, than the accomplished British sailor. But the circumstances of his profession, resembling in many respects those of the land-officer, lead to a disregard of prudence and sobriety, and all those unostentatious virtues of economy, which, in the exuberant generosity of his noble heart, he is apt to despise as narrow, spiritless, and unbecoming his character. The consequence, however, of neglecting them, must of necessity be the same in all professions, embarrassment, distress, ill health, and uneasy reflection.

I have now, according to my design, taken a cursory view of the four professions; those of divinity, of physic, of law, and of arms. I have endeavoured to point out a few evils, which the *circumstances* at-

tending each of them have a natural tendency to
produce; and this I have done, not with the malignant purpose of exposing or reviling them, but
with the well-intended aim of admonishing young
men of the danger, that it may be more easily
avoided.

To confirm my idea that particular professions are
subject to peculiar errors, arising from their *circumstances*, I shall close the subject with quoting a passage from Dr. Powel's Discourse on the Vices incident to an Academical Life.

'There are,' says he, ' writers of some reputation
in physic, who have undertaken to explain, to what
particular diseases men are exposed by each profession and employment. Whatever their success has
been, their design was certainly good; and if the attempt is not too difficult, it will be useful to pursue
the same plan in our moral inquiries. We frequently
exhort every man to observe with care the com-
plexion and temper of his soul, and to apply all such
remedies as may either prevent or palliate those disorders to which his natural constitution makes him
subject. But every man is not able to judge of his
own dispositions; and what we call nature, is more
often habit. It would be well, therefore, if we could
assist the diligent searcher of his heart, by shewing
him what vices usually accompany his situation and
circumstances. He will more easily discover his own
personal character, if he is acquainted with that of
the rank or order to which he belongs.

' Very little pains have been employed by any
moral writers to this purpose. They have told us,
perhaps, what are the faults of youth and of age,
what the dangers of riches and of poverty; but if
any thing has been said concerning the characters
of particular professions, it has been by the satirist,
not the serious moralists.'

Let me be permitted to adopt his conclusion, and apply it to my preceding observations.

'Ought we not, therefore, it may be asked, to fly from stations where our virtue and our happiness are exposed to so many dangers? Alas! whither shall we fly? What place, what scene of life can promise us security? Each condition is surrounded with different indeed, but almost equal, difficulties. Each, too, has its peculiar advantages to compensate those difficulties, and possibly none may have greater than our own. Nor are the foregoing observations to be understood so strictly, as if they never failed in any instance. Let it not be imagined that the faults incident to an order, must necessarily adhere to all the individuals who compose it. Few are so unfortunate as to be hit by every weapon which the enemy aims against them. And some, perhaps either by the natural activity and vigour of their minds, may avoid, or with the shield of reason and religion, may repel them all. If this were impossible, the inquiry in which we have been engaged would be useless. These reflections can serve no other purpose, but that, knowing to what vices our situation inclines us, we may, by continual efforts and firm resolutions, bend all our faculties towards the opposite virtues; and having extricated ourselves "from the sins which most easily beset us," may run with patience the race that is set before us.'

NUMBER XXXVI.

On the Amusement of Archery, and other Diversions.
Ev. 36.

As in every opulent and peaceful country, a great part of mankind live in the world principally to take

their pastime in it; it is happy when a taste prevails
for such amusements, as, while they add grace,
health, and vigour to the body, have no tendency
to enfeeble and corrupt the mind. The revival of
archery has lately received the sanction of fashion;
and fortunately, it is a diversion which deserves, at the
same time, the approbation of reason. It is manly,
without partaking of ferocity; it is pleasing, though,
at the same time, most remote from the pleasures
of effeminacy. It deserves encouragement, that it
may counteract, on one hand, the prevalence of a
pugilistic taste; and, on the other, of an enervating
delight in domestic games of chance.

The amusement of tennis ought also to be encouraged, as an exercise; since it is capable of being
enjoyed in the worst weather, and the worst seasons;
and in England there is so much bad weather, and
so long a winter, that archery can be pursued but
for a short time in the whole year. Tennis, or the
pilæ ludus, is truly a classical game; highly esteemed
by the most respectable Greeks and Romans; mentioned by Homer, Herodotus, Pliny, Horace; and
recommended by Galen as one of the most salutary
exercises. It ought not to be forgotten that the ball,
the little implement which has afforded so much
health and pleasure, is said to have been invented
by Aganella, a beautiful young lady of Corcyra, who
presented the first she ever made, with directions
how to use it, to the princess Nausicaa, the daughter
of Alcinous. Whether it required much genius to
invent it, is a disquisition into which I shall not enter, lest it should terminate in detraction from the
beautiful Aganella. Her memory is entitled to be a
toast of the cricketers and tennis players, without
any such invidious inquiry.

Hawking was once as much in fashion as archery
is at present. No country gentleman could well

maintain his right to that character without a hawk on his fist. But it was an expensive, a dangerous, and a troublesome diversion. The sportsmen, while their eyes were fixed on the birds in the air, often found themselves plunged into a ditch or a horse-pond.

There is a pretty diversion said, in the Relations of Sir Anthony Sherlies, to have been followed by the Persian kings, which may be called *hawking in miniature.* Sparrows, instead of hawks, are *reclaimed,* as the term is, or broken in, and taught to fly after butterflies, and bring them to their masters. If our English sparrows could be rendered equally docile, which I much doubt, it would be a delightful summer amusement for the ladies of the flower-gardens, and a very useful employment for those students in natural history, who admire and collect insects of the papilionaceous tribe.

Angling seems never to have been a very fashionable amusement, though very ardently pursued by its votaries. Some degree of cruelty attending it, has contributed to bring it into disrepute. It requires a great degree of stillness, silence, patience; and a skill and discernment in times, seasons, waters, baits, weather, and many minute articles which fashionable people of pleasure are not very willing to exercise. For the consolation of anglers I will cite a passage on their art from Burton's Anatomy of Melancholy. 'Plutarch,' says he, ' speaks against all fishing, as a filthy, base, illiberal employment, having neither wit nor perspicacity in it, nor worth the labour. But he that shall consider the variety of baits for all seasons, and the pretty devices which our anglers have invented, peculiar lines, false flies, several sleights, &c. will say that it deserves like commendation, requires as much study and perspicacity as the rest, and is to be preferred before many of them; because hawking and hunting are very laborious; much riding, and many dangers, accompany them; but this is still and quiet; and *if so be* the angler catch no fish, yet he hath a wholesome walk by the brook side, pleasant shade by the sweet silver streams; he hath good air, and sweet smells of fine fresh meadow flowers; he hears the melodious harmony of birds; he sees the swans, herons, and many other fowl, with their brood, which he thinketh better than the noise of hounds, or blast of horns, and all the sport that they can make.'

Angling certainly excites the hopes and fears of those who pursue it earnestly, as much as any other of the sports; and therefore answers all the purposes of rural diversion: and as to the charge of cruelty, I am afraid none of the sports are more entitled to an exemption from it. Angling, however, on many accounts, is not likely to become a fashionable sport; and is justly called, in the title of the best book upon it, the Contemplative Man's Recreation. It is conducted in silence and solitude; it makes no ostentatious appearance; it seldom displays agility, grace, or strength, and therefore is not accommodated to the views of those, who seek their pleasure in the eyes of their observers.

To archery no cruelty can be objected. Nothing is killed; nothing is hunted. There is in it trial of skill which excites a pleasing emulation; and hope and fear are gently, and therefore agreeably, agitated. There is also an elegance in the instruments, and a pleasing imitation of old English manners in the dress and appearance of the bowmen. I think it probable that the nation will soon have a large army of archers, and I wish it may have no occasion for any other.

The revival of a taste for archery has revived an attention to an old book which used to sleep on the shelves, and to be disturbed by none but a few lite-rary virtuosi; the Toxophilus of Ascham. It has of late been much read by those who hoped to improve their skill in the management of the bow and arrow, by its instructions. In this, I believe, they have been disappointed. Manual dexterity is chiefly im-proved by practice. Theory and written directions oftener puzzle than explain, when they are applied to arts which are most effectually advanced to per-fection, by what is called a knack, or an habitual facility derived from repeated and mechanical ex-perience.

But Ascham's book deserves the attention of the scholar, not only as a curious, but as an excellent specimen; for excellent it may be proved, if the time of its appearance is taken into consideration. Ascham formed his style on the model of the an-cients. Accustomed to write Latin, he caught the rhythm of classical composition, and transferred it to his own language. He made a great effort in reaching the excellence he attained; since his own country afforded him no good models. He who, under such disadvantages, could write so good a style, must have been possessed of extraordinary ability. But though I deem his style excellent as an imitation of the ancients, and as an early effort in English literature; yet, I am sensible, that those who have been only conversant with the polished language of later writers, will condemn it as stiff, formal, awkward, and pedantic. It has, on many occasions, a just right to these epithets. Yet, on the other hand, it is strong, forcible, nervous, and emphatic. But when I number him among the suc-cessful imitators of the ancients, I mean that he is such an imitator as that builder would be, who after seeing the marble remains of antiquity at Rome, should come home and erect structures, similar in form, with brick or with wooden materials. Ascham's Schoolmaster is, in many parts, more eloquent than his Toxophilus.

The Toxophilus of Ascham suggests an idea that the author was himself a great lover of the bow and arrow. But I think it rather doubtful, whether so severe a scholar was greatly addicted to an amusement, which, however it was honoured at court, was considered in those times as too light and trifling for a scholar. I rather think poor Ascham wrote solely on this subject from the mercenary motive of attaining a pension from the eighth Henry. There are several passages in his letters which led directly to this surmise. 'I wrote my Toxophilus' says he, 'not so much with a design to do honour to archery, or to direct the practice of it, as to try the experiment, whether the treatise might not improve my circumstances, which are low indeed, lower than the common condition of the studious; for I found that several persons had received very great favours from his Majesty, as rewards for their skill in archery[*].'

Ascham was not disappointed. The King gave him a pension of ten pounds a year, estimated as equivalent to a hundred at the present period. It is a melancholy reflection, that he might have lived and died in extreme penury, notwithstanding his great merits in various departments of learning, if he had not sagaciously written on a subject which drew the attention of the king, and gratified his pre-

* Scripsi ego Toxophilum meum, non tam quod honestatem sagittationis et ejus usum scripto me illustrare instituerim, quam potissimum, ut hâc viâ insisterem, periculum facturus, num ea aliquando vitæ meæ rationes *tenues admodum*, et infra communem studiosorum conditionem positas promovere potuerit: intellexi enim aliquot peritos sagittarios summa beneficia a regiâ majestate accepisse.—— Lib. ii.

There are other passages in his letters nearly to the same purpose.

vailing taste. Ascham, in this instance, proved himself a good toxophilite. He took a good aim, shot with strength and skill, and fixed his arrow in the target. All honest bowmen must wish that he had lived to enjoy his good fortune longer. But he was a valetudinarian, like most of the laborious students of his day, and died at fifty-three. Had he practised the art which he commended a little more, he probably would have enjoyed better health, and might have lived to produce books far superior to his Toxophilus and his Schoolmaster.

But to return from the old treatise on archery, to the practice of it in the present age. The ladies seem to be ambitious of shooting darts, in a literal sense, as they have long been celebrated for doing execution by their figurative artillery. Above the childish bow and arrow of little Cupid, they take the weapons of the warrior, and emulate the prowess of Robin Hood and Ulysses. *Venus armed*, has been the subject of several ancient and modern epigrams. The wits, however, tell us that she never conquers in arms; but that she is invincible when she approaches unarmed, and clad in native beauty. They intended, I believe, to explode the affectation of masculine dress, manners, and diversions, which has of late greatly predominated in the circles of fashion. Women wear beaver hats and broad-cloth coats like men; women hunt* and sometimes shoot, not arrows only, but powder and shot; there are female jockeys, female swearers, female gamesters, female drinkers, and why, in this improving age, should there not be female boxers? The Roman emperors encouraged female gladiators; and there are features in modern times not unlike those of the Romans.

* Mævia Tuscum
     Figit aprum—— Juv.
    Mævia hunts the Tuscan boar.

T 2

emperors. It is worth remarking, that before a lady can be perfectly well qualified for archery, or any other manly exercise of the belligerent kind, she must prepare herself, like the ancient Amazons, by the painful amputation of a beautiful part, the absence of which, no masculine dress can compensate. Venus, Hebe, Cupid, and the Graces, swoon at the very idea of this amputation: but Alecto, Megæra, and Tisiphone, make all hell resound with their plaudits, and grin horribly a ghastly smile of complacency at the hope of seeing their own deformity rendered less conspicuous by the crowd of their imitators. Their imitators have set a fashion of deformity; and all that is sweet in delicacy, and captivating in feminine grace, is hastening to follow it.

NUMBER XXXVII.

On Fastidious Conversation.—Ev. 37.

THERE are persons so extremely refined and so delicately nice, that conversation, as it is commonly conducted, even among the sensible and well-bred, affords them but little pleasure; and as it appears among people in the middle rank, persons of plain sense and simple manners, actually puts them to *ineffable* torture.

This fastidiousness of conversation, where it is *real*, though valued as a high distinction, and the cause of pride in those who possess it, is a great misfortune. The perfection which it expects is not to be found in this sublunary state; and in pursuit of it, disappointment is constantly incurred. In the ous intercourse of life, the company of all sorts of people must sometimes be engaged in, and the majority may perhaps be inelegant, injudicious, and absurd; but still a really good understanding will make due allowance for defect of natural ability, defect of education, defect of good examples, and a hundred other defects, which must render conversation, as it is commonly met with in the world, very far from perfect. Good sense, united with good nature, and subdued to candour by experience, will find, amidst all these defects, something to afford pleasure, and something to contribute toward knowledge and improvement.

But this fastidiousness is oftener affected than real; and it is the *manner* of conversation which causes this disgust more frequently than the matter; for common sense is distributed without partiality to the majority of mankind in every rank of society. The artificial and refined modes of expressing it are indeed confined to those classes, whose opulence affords a superior education, and whose situation enables them to catch the transient graces of the prevailing fashion. But this refinement often weakens while it polishes. And the plain common sense of ordinary people, forms a solid, massy ore, which men of sense will prize, notwithstanding the dirt and extraneous matter with which it may be encumbered. But the over-refined and over-delicate cannot stoop to pick up the most precious jewel from a dunghill. The jewel must be set in gold, and presented in a costly casket, or they turn away from it with expressions of disdain. They will not take even gold and silver, if it is the common currency. They must traffic with pearls and diamonds, or with something else, if it is possible, still more exquisite.

But to the fastidious, not merely the vulgar, but those of liberal education and polite manners, are causes of *squeamishness*, if they are deficient in cer-

tain little graces, or modes of behaviour, which are
no more to solid sense and goodness of heart, than
the shell of the nut is to the kernel. 'Mr. Such-a-
one,' says one of the over-delicate fraternity or sis-
terhood, 'is a very learned and good man, to be
sure. Much may be learned from him. He is very
entertaining to many, and not deficient in good
nature and civility; but I know not how it is, I
cannot bear his conversation: it is so unlike the
fashionable ton of Sir Versatile Varnish. It wants
a *je ne scai quoi;* that *indescribable something* which
I believe is visible only to the purged eye of people
of fashion. Sir Versatile Varnish is, to be sure, no
scholar. He wrote us a letter the other day, with
bad spelling and false grammar; but he has the art
of pleasing in conversation. You never think it
worth while to remember any thing he says: but
you listen to him while he speaks, and you are
charmed. Mr. ———— is all that science and experience can contribute towards making a learned, a
sensible, a wise, and a virtuous man; but he is
awkward, and I cannot admit him to habits of familiarity. No; we must not visit him; but, however,
we shall be at no loss for company, since Sir Versatile will be here very often, and Seignior ————,
and Monsieur ————, have promised to spend a
month or two with us, to enliven our summer residence at the dull mote in Hertfordshire.'

The contempt for good and sensible people who
have not the *indescribable something* in conversation,
becomes in time a degree of inveterate hatred,
which no human creature should harbour towards
another. The proud treat them, for want of the
indescribable something, as if they were of another
species; and look down upon them, much as the
imperious manager of a plantation looks down upon
the negroes under his whip; and with far less esteem

than the fastidious gentleman and lady behold their pointers, their greyhounds, their hunters, and their lap-dogs.

Indeed this excessive delicacy originates more frequently in excessive self-conceit, and excessive ill-nature, than from any excessive superiority of taste, or excessive discernment. The pride of the pretenders to it is flattered, and their malice gratified, in finding something in every one, who has the misfortune to converse with them, wrong, defective, and disagreeable.

No virtue, no excellence, moral or intellectual, no beauty, no innocence, can be secured from the malignant satire of persons who have once persuaded themselves that they have an *indescribable something* in their own persons, understandings, and manners, superior to the rest of mankind. Their whole delight and chief employment, as soon as their company is gone, is to ridicule and blame the behaviour and character of every one whom they had just caressed and entertained at their tables, with Judas-like smiles, and dissembled hospitality; which, it must be confessed, is an *indescribable* baseness.

The persons most liable to this folly, in both sexes, are smatterers in literature, would-be wits, and half-bred people of fashion. Not furnished with a sufficient stock of real merit to rise by their own elasticity, they have no means of viewing themselves on the elevation they aspire at but depressing all around them.

There is, indeed, so much affectation of superior taste, delicacy, and refinement; and it leads to such unmanly, unchristian, ungenerous treatment of others, that every man of solid understanding, who at the same time possesses a due sense of esteem for the human species, however unimproved in arts, must wish to discourage it, by denying it that respect and attention which its vanity claims as its due.

A microscopic eye for the discovery of defects and ugliness, is surely not desirable. If a power of vision so accurate and minute, is cultivated and acquired, let it be chiefly exerted in discovering the latent good qualities of our fellow-creatures; the integrity, the genius, and virtue of every kind which often lies concealed under a forbidding outside, and escapes the notice of these pretenders to extraordinary discernment.

It is indeed impossible but that superior understanding, improved by the advantages of a liberal education, and the company of the learned, the polished, and the experienced, should see defects in those who have not enjoyed these benefits. But their superiority of understanding will teach them to make allowances for unavoidable blemishes; and not to be implacably offended at little errors, deficiencies in forms, and neglect of decorum arising from ignorance or inattention; at natural failings or deformities, to which themselves or their families are liable, as well as others, or at any thing else where no offence is intended. Such a conduct will be no less politic than benevolent; for he who is offended at others, commonly offends them; and creates a busy and vigilant enmity which will usually find, at some time or other, opportunities for severe retaliation.

It is the good-natured advice of Horace, that instead of magnifying and aggravating the faults of those with whom we converse, we should extenuate them, by giving them gentle appellations, just as a father palliates the bodily deformities of his child, by calling them pretty oddities, and lovely little deviations from the common ordinary standard of nature. It is certain that the unaffected suavity of disposition which bears with involuntary error, and employs itself to find out excellences to counterbalance faults in characters, contributes more to personal happiness and the comforts of society, than the acutest sagacity, malignantly employed in detecting and describing little blemishes and trifling deviations from the fluctuating standard of fashion.

NUMBER XXXVIII.

On some of the old Sermon Writers.—Ev. 38.

IT was the great misfortune of the old sermon writers, that they were obliged, by the fashion of their time, to preach an hour at least, and, on extraordinary occasions, much longer. Instead of compressing their subject, they were compelled by custom tediously to dilate it. They beat out their little gold, till it became a useless leaf; they spun their thread to such a degree of tenuity, that it became as subtile and as worthless as a cobweb.

The facetious Dr. Eachard relates of an old preacher, that he took for his text, ' But his delight is in the law of the Lord.' He observed, that every word was significant and expressive. ' To begin with the first word, *but*. This *but*,' says he, ' is full of good wine; we will broach it, and taste a little—then proceed.'

This instance, I imagine, is either feigned or exaggerated, to serve the purpose of the jocular writer; but it really gives no improper idea of the method which the old sermonizers pursued to eke out their sermons to their ordinary and most grievous dimensions.

The celebrated Dr. Donne thus begins a ser-

mon* on the text, ' And without controversy great
is the mystery of godliness.'

' This is no text for an hour-glass; if God would
afford me Hezekiah's sign, *ut revertatur umbra*, that
the shadow might go back upon the dial; or Joshua's
sign, *ut sistat sol*, that the sun might stand still all
the day, this were text enough to employ all the
day, and all the days of our life. The lent which
we begin now, is a full tithe of the year; but the
hour which we begin now is not a full tithe of this
day, and therefore we should not grudge all that.
But payment of tithes is become matter of controversy; and we, by our text, are directed to matters
without controversy. And without controversy great
is the mystery of godliness.'

Such is the exordium of the preacher, and without controversy it must have been a very comfortable hearing to a shivering congregation, in the
season of Lent, on the sixteenth of February. The
quaint nonsense of the exordium thus promising a
long discourse, was at least an admonition to the congregation to summon all their patience. Well might
Mr. Boyle write a consolatory Essay on long sermons. He seems to allow an hour as a reasonable
time; but the great object, in his days, seems to
have been to gain the character of a fine preacher,
not by quality, but by quantity of matter.

Let me be permitted to cite one or two other specimens from the same sermon of Dr. Donne. ' Must
I be damned?' says he, ' the evidence of my salvation is my *credo*, not their *probo*; and if I must get
to heaven by syllogism, my major is, *credo in Deum
Patrem*, I believe in God the Father; for Pater,
major, the Father is greater than all; and my *minor*
shall be *credo in Deum Filium*, I believe in God the
Son, *qui exivit de Patre*, he came from God; and
my conclusion, which must proceed from major and

* Preached before the king, at Whitehall, February 16, 1620.

minor, shall be *credo in Spiritum Sanctum*, I believe in the Holy Ghost, who proceeds from Father and Son; and this syllogism brought me into the militant church at my baptism, and this will carry me into the triumphant, in my transmigration; for doctrine of salvation is matter *without controversy.*

This curious argumentation takes its rise from the words *without controversy* in the text, which probably mean no more than *without doubt*; but the taking of the words of the text, and descanting upon them separately, served the two-fold purpose of filling up the hour, and of obtaining the praise of *sticking to the text*, for the accomplishment of which the preacher would not stick at the most far-fetched absurdity of explication.

Dr. Donne was a man of great wit, sense, and learning. Nothing but the unfortunate fashion of dilating on words, merely to fill up the time, could have led him to preach in a quaint unnatural manner, very nearly approaching to the nonsensical.

I will do him the justice to cite a passage with which he concludes the sermon, from which the above sentences are extracted.

' And because God dwells *in luce inaccessibili*, in a glorious light, which you cannot see here, glorify him in that in which you may see him, in that wherein he hath manifested himself, glorify him in his glorious gospel: employ your beams of glory, honour, favour, fortune, in transmitting the same glory to your children, as you received it from your fathers, for in this consists the mystery of godliness, which is faith with a pure conscience.' *O si sic omnia!*

But he begins his next sermon with a passage, which again seems to be a demand from the pulpit, for patience: The text is, ' For where your treasure is, there will your heart be also.' Alluding to the hour-glass, which stood by his side, he says, ' If I had a secular glass, a glass that would run an age.

if the two hemispheres of the world were composed in the form of such a glass, and all the world calcined and burnt to ashes, and all the ashes, and sands, and atoms of the world put into that glass, it would not be enough to tell the godly man, what his treasure, and the object of his heart is.'

He proceeds thus a little lower : ' Our text stands as that proverbial, that hieroglyphical Pythagoras's Y ; that hath first a stalk, a stem to fix itself, and then spreads into two beams. The stem, the stalk of this letter, this Y in the first word of the text, is that particle of argumentation, *for* . . . . and then opens this symbolical, this cabalistical letter, this Y, into two horns, two beams, two branches ; one broader, but on the left hand, denoting the treasures of the world ; the other narrower, but on the right hand, denoting treasure laid up for the world to come. Be sure you turn the right way.'—Here we see the hammer of the gold-beater, working hard on the anvil, to produce a film.

It must be owned, however, that many of these old writers abound with ideas, which, though they violate decorum and are greatly strained, yet afford much entertainment to a curious reader ; entertainment resulting not only from their oddity, but their ingenuity. One might make a considerable collection from them of witty remarks, approaching to *bon mots*. The modern writer, though infinitely more elegant and decorous, is often insipid on comparison. The old writers laboured hard to produce matter from their own brain, which, though often flimsy as Arachne's web, had the merit of ingenious originality. They often snatched a grace, by venturing to say daring things ; things that advanced on the very brink of impropriety ; but the modern is restrained and cooled by caution or timidity. The refined congregations of the present day would not tolerate such adventurous thoughts, such hazardous expressions, such approaches to downright burlesque and nonsense. The awe of an audience checks the preacher, like tying the wings of an eagle.

Whoever wishes to entertain himself with the quaintness of the old sermon writers, will find a fund of such entertainment, as he seeks, in the sermons of Bishop Andrews, Barten Halliday, Gataker, Donne, Saunderson, South, and many others of the last century. At the same time, he will discover in them a rich mine of fine sense often well expressed; and a vein of piety, simplicity, and godly sincerity, which no awkwardness of manner and expression can ever depreciate.

But to the honour of the present race of divines, it must be acknowledged, that they greatly excel their predecessors in preserving the decorum and dignity of the pulpit. They exhibit a gravity and modesty which peculiarly becomes the chaste matron, Religion. Their decent mode of preaching, raises a respectable attention to their doctrine, far more favourable to the advancement of religion, than learning sullied with pedantry, exhortation vulgarized by low wit, argument perplexed by scholastic subtilty, exposition spoiled by quaintness, and pious declamation rendered ludicrous by humour and ill-placed pleasantry.

NUMBER XXXIX.

On the Inconsistences of Avarice, and on petty Avarice.—Ev. 39.

FROM a strange inconsistency in the human mind, it sometimes happens that men who are sufficiently generous and bountiful on great occasions, disgrace

and distress themselves by a parsimony in such trifles as are utterly unworthy of their care. This mean
part of the character, the overvaluing of trifles, has
not escaped that accurate observer of the living world,
Theophrastus. He has described the quality which
forms it, under the denomination of MICROLOGIA, or
that species of avarice which estimates little things
greatly above their own value; or which notices minute articles which are beneath its regard.

He enumerates several instances of this petty nig-
gardliness, more applicable indeed to his own times
than to ours, but yet such as modern manners too often resemble. Among many other specimens of this
narrowness, he mentions that his Micrologus, when
at a public feast, or perhaps at a dinner at his own
house, instead of being engaged by the conversation,
attends solely to reckoning how many glasses each
of the guests has drunk, and computing arithmetically
how many bottles are on the whole exhausted.

The ancient satirists and comic writers* are very
severe and facetious on this sordid disposition. Plautus, describing a *petty miser,* for so I shall term the
man of this character, gives us to understand, that
when his nails have been cut by the operator, whom
the moderns would call a chiropodist, he carefully
wraps up the parings, and hugging himself with the

---

* Casaubon, in his notes to the chapter on the Micrologia in
Theophrastus, has collected a number of curious appellations
which the Greek writers give to the *petty miser.* They are similar
to those of the English *skin-flint, split-farthing, nip-cheese, pinch-
penny, close-fist, hold-fast, gripe;* from which we may conclude,
that this irrational character was always common, and always the
subject of comic ridicule. As to ridicule, the miser always said
in his heart,

    Populus me sibilat—at mihi plaudo
    Ipse domi—simul ac nummos contemplor in arcâ.—Hor.

Casaubon refers to this passage in Plautus, whence the ideas in
the subsequent description are taken.

consciousness of his treasure, pockets the precious deposit, and walks off with an air of perfect self-complacency. When he washes his hands, he laments with a sigh, that so much water must be thrown away. If he sees a little smoke issuing from his chimney, he grieves, as if his house were on fire; and cannot help thinking it is a pity so much good smoke should be lost in the air, which would have served to smoke the flich of bacon, if it had happily been confined within doors. By these strokes of hyperbole, the poet means to hint that such men cannot bear to part with any thing, not only not the parings, but not even the dirt under their nails*. The character has always afforded a fine topic for comedy and farce; but I am not sure that it ought not to be viewed with pity rather than derision, as it appears to resemble insanity.

Yet some men of enlightened minds and singular liberality of ideas, have exhibited in their conduct strange instances of petty parsimony. Paper is an article, which, considering its utility and beauty, may be deemed cheap; yet some who are able to make the best use of it, by filling it with good sense, wit, poetry, and eloquence, have been niggards of it in the extreme.

That accurate observer, Swift, gave Pope the epithet of *paper-saving*; which he certainly deserved, for I have seen, in the British Museum, some of his manuscripts written on the covers of letters, so closely, as almost to confound the lines of the poet with the superscription.

Chapelain, a polite and famous scholar of France, was expected, from his connexion with Voiture and Balzac, to leave behind him many letters of great elegance. But they were found, on examination, unworthy of the public eye; and it was assigned as a reason, that Chapelain being of the *paper-saving* class,

* Ne *gry* quidem.

studied nothing in writing his letters, but to make them as short as possible, that he might save a bit of paper. It is a wonder that these parsimonious scribes did not omit dots and tittles to save ink.

Petty parsimony is very common in the articles of stationery. Many write in so small a character, and so closely, to spare paper, that it is impossible to decipher their manuscripts. Many dilute their ink till it is thin and pale as water, and soon becomes yellow as saffron, or vanishes and leaves not a trace behind. Many wear their pens to stumps as little fit for writing as a skewer. Many grudge wax enough to secure their letter from opening in its passage by the post from London to Islington, and treasure up a wafer with as much care as a guinea. All these, at the same time, shall be rich enough to keep equipages, and villas, and to indulge in every delight of expensive luxury.

Some there are who had rather not hear from their best friends and nearest relations, than pay the postage of a letter; who are perpetually engaged in broils with carriers, stage-coachmen, hackney-coachmen, watermen, and porters, about overcharges of a penny or two-pence, though the time they spend, and the uneasiness they feel in the dispute, are such, as pounds could not compensate; and after all, the sum in debate is of no more consequence to them than the dust on their shoes, or the powder in their perukes. Add to which, that they usually have the worst of it in the result; their foolish parsimony being such, as to lead them to refuse payment when it is due, and can be legally exacted.

The *petty miser* is sure to pick a personal quarrel with the tax-gatherer; and treats all persons who come with a legal demand for money due to others, as if they came to make unjustifiable claims upon him for their own advantage. He goes to his country-house at Hackney for the benefit of the air, but has stopped up more than half the windows in it out of spite to Mr. Pitt. He found that the stoppage of two windows more would save a crown a year; and therefore, notwithstanding the remonstrances of his wife and daughter, he plastered up the bow-window, and one of the side sashes in the drawing-room.

If the *petty miser* goes on a party of pleasure, or a rural excursion, he spoils all the comfort of it by suffering his temper to be ruffled by quarrels with post-chaise boys, waiters, boot-catchers, or turnpike-men, about pence and halfpence. Though he has spent many pounds in the excursion, he comes home without having received the pleasure he pursued; because he lost the power of being pleased, in losing his temper in controversies for sums amounting, perhaps, in the whole, to half a crown.

The petty miser is extremely penurious in all the articles of dress. He will not lay aside a coat, or a hat, till they are quite worn out, though the very boys laugh at his ludicrous appearance, as he passes along the streets. In a public mourning, he brings out a quondam black coat, which was new at the death of Queen Anne, and has now undergone a curious change of colour, like the leaves in autumn; and from a raven-gray, is become a bottle-green. His servants, in the mean time, are clad in as good liveries as those of other people.

If he is caught in a shower, in returning from the Bank, where he has received a large dividend, he will not call a coach, or stop at a coffee-house, but stands an hour or two under a gateway, and at last trudges home in the rain, with such a cold and sore-throat, and a wig so much injured, that the emulsions and reparations cost more than the coach would have amounted to, if it had been hired for the whole day; but he looks with delight at the shilling he saved, and triumphs in the wisdom of his economy.

If he gives a pittance, which is but rare, to an importunate petitioner, or to persons who collect for a charity, or for the lecturer of the parish, he throws it down with so ill a grace, and with so many murmurs at the multitude of taxes and the hardness of the times, that the receivers feel themselves hurt at the gift, and would gladly go without the money to escape the unpleasant rencounter. At the same time he subscribes liberally to the relief of debtors confined for small debts, and to the Asylum.

In the months of January and February, he sits shivering by a fire, which you might cover with your hand; though he is racked with a rheumatism, which a warm room would relieve, and though, in every other apartment in his house, the fires are as large as those who sit by them choose to make them. He does not begin fires till the first of November, and ends them on the last day of March; because it was the good old custom of his family, and good old customs should never be laid aside. Nobody chooses to come near him at these cold periods, and his fingers and feet swell with chilblains; but he does not mind that, as he is keeping up a good old custom.

When he is ill, instead of seeking the advice of an apothecary or physician, he prescribes for himself from Buchan's Domestic Medicine, or an old family receipt-book of his grandmother's, and buys a pennyworth of drugs at the shop, which he administers to himself, in consequence of which he has brought on disorders which nearly cost him his life, and, at the same time, large sums in daily and long-repeated fees to the doctor. But notwithstanding this, he is an annual contributor to more than one dispensary, established for supplying the poor with medicine and advice gratuitously.

I believe he is of the same species as the miser Hopkins, celebrated by Mr. Pope; for, though he is always very saving of candles-ends during his life, he is attended with numerous torches at his funeral, being sumptuously buried by the heir who is so much benefited by his parsimonious life.

The inconsistent miser, who places too high a value on trifles, and yet is as free as others in some parts of his expenses, is a curious, but no uncommon, phenomenon. It is caused by want of reasoning, by thoughtlessness of a peculiar kind, by early habits of meanness acquired before the fortune was made, and at a time when little things were really important. This early association is not easily corrected in old age, or even in manhood; and he, to whom a pair of shoes or a coat were things of prime consequence, when he was an apprentice, a clerk, or a porter, can scarcely help thinking them equally so, when his industry and virtue have clothed him in scarlet, put a gold chain round his neck, and seated him in the coach of the Lord Mayor.

I should be gratified, if any of these hints might correct the error, which often poisons the sweets of good fortune, and renders men of singular integrity, industry, fidelity, and even partial generosity, the objects of hatred to those whom their petty avarice pinches, and of supreme contempt to the common observer.

NUMBER XL.

On artful, prostituted, and excessive Praise.—Ev. 40.

THE prostitution of praise, for venal purposes, is a species of deception which deserves to be ranked among the frauds of the vilest depredator on property. It robs virtue of the best among its sublunary rewards, and bestows it on crafty villany, on plausible ignorance, on hypocritical pretence; on every character, however idle, useless, and worthless, which is at the same time subtle enough to wear a mask to save appearances, and can join, with an air of gravity, in the interested collusion. I do not at present comprehend flattery under the prostitution of praise of which I am speaking; but merely that practice of extolling men beyond measure, to serve their interest, which is known by the cant name of *puffing;* a name good enough indeed for the thing signified; but a name which implies something as far beneath real praise, as Dr. Rock, of notorious memory, was inferior to that honour of human nature, Dr. Heberden.

When a parent dwells with rapture on the genius and improvements of a lubberly lad, and a lover expatiates with ecstasy on beauties in his mistress which she does not possess, few can be deceived; because the world is sagacious enough to discover, and good-natured enough to make allowances for, the blind partiality of immoderate affection.

But honest affection, and blind and mistaken partiality, have no concern in the prostitution of praise, which I at present contemplate. This originates in low cunning, and is compatible with sovereign contempt for the very object which it extols to the skies.

The artful puffer is a philosopher of the Chesterfieldian school. His great object is to make the world his *bubble*. He is perfectly acquainted with the best methods of sporting the puff-selfish, and can throw in even censure itself in such an adroit manner, as to contribute ultimately to his praise. He has a thousand arts in conversation, acquired by studying the great founder of the sect, which tend to set off his paltry beads and French paste, and make them mistaken for real pearls, and diamonds of the first water. But I intend only to view him at present as the puffer of others, of his relations, friends, patrons, and of all others by whom some selfish purpose is to be accomplished, his interest advanced, his vanity tickled, or his pride, either personal or of family, indulged.

The puffer, we will suppose, has a cousin, or a brother, or a common acquaintance, who, stimulated by the hope of gain or preferment, has produced an abortive poem, or a ricketty treatise in prose. The finest type and paper has been used; plates inserted by the most eminent artists; copies sent free of carriage, and all bound and lettered in the manner of Baumgarten, to many great people, famous critics, eminent literati; yet all in vain. The ill-formed bantling cannot stand upon its legs. Puffing is as necessary, as the bellows of the Humane Society, to resuscitate the expiring corpse. To work, therefore, the puffing professor goes, with all the zeal of an operator who expects to receive the silver medal.

'Have you seen,' he asks in all companies to which he can gain access, 'have you seen the excellent Poem, or Dissertation, which has such a run, and which some attribute to Mr. A. or Dr. B.?—My God, Sir, it is a fine performance. The language so elegant, the ideas so new; the—the—in short, buy it. It will be a standard book. But I must not leave you under the mistake of its being the production of Mr. A. or Dr. B.: it is, to let you into a great secret, it is the work of my cousin; as promising a young man, I suppose, as any in the three kingdoms. O my God, Sir, it is astonishing what parts he possesses. He wrote this excellent book off-hand—mere play to him. He is idle—the dog is idle—a fault of all great geniuses—but then he has no occasion for plodding. Depend upon it, he will make a great figure; and be soon at the head of his profession in rank, as he is in merit, and has been some time, notwithstanding his youth.'

If a friend of his brings out a play, more soporific than the dullest sermon, he declares that the house overflowed, and that it was received with repeated bursts of applause; though the few that were there, were admitted by orders; and every one of them caught sore throats by the chill blasts that blew through the empty rows of the pit, boxes, and gallery.

He goes to a charity sermon at a crowded chapel, where his nephew holds forth, in consequence of his suggesting that a young man should put himself forward in the world, or else he will be neglected and starve. The poor nephew has the misfortune to have an impediment in his speech, forces what little he can articulate through the nasal orifices, and is obliged to that great professor of theology, Dr. Trusler, for all his divinity. It is true, the congregation grumble, and very few shillings jingle in the churchwardens' plate at the door; but the puffing professor intends that his nephew shall stand for a neighbouring lectureship then vacant, and therefore he sallies forth, and informs all that he can take the liberty of speaking to in the parish, that he really was never better entertained in his whole life, than he was with the discourse of a mighty pretty young man, who preached a charity sermon at Fashion-street chapel this morning. There was in it all the perspicuity of Tillotson, and all the solidity of Clarke, united with the florid elegance of Seed, the pathos of Sterne, and the copious fluency of Blair. 'O, my God, Sir, he was great indeed. Nothing theatrical neither in his manner. No, no; nothing but the plain, dignified simplicity, which is the best garb of religion. A most excellent preacher! It is not the lot of every one to wear a mitre; but it is more glorious to deserve it. A very flattering circumstance to myself it is, that I have the honour to call this most promising young divine my near relation.'

He has another friend or relation a painter. 'Have you been to the Exhibition?' O yes. 'Then, I hope you took due notice of the best picture in the room, Mr. Le Daub's portrait of that most excellent preacher, my nephew, the prebendary, that preached the famous sermon, that made so much noise, some years back, at Fashion-street chapel. Indeed you could not but be struck with it. The original is as fine a figure, I suppose, as ever existed, and the picture has done it justice indeed; ample justice; for it breathes, it speaks—my God, it is too much—art has outstripped nature. The resemblance is actually more like nature than the living original; all life, fire, and energy. Poor Sir Joshua! it was unlucky for you that Le Daub's picture was hung up so near your feeble attempts. Le Daub, I suppose, bids fair to be the greatest portrait painter this country ever beheld. But he has too much business. People of fashion will be painted by nobody else now.'

His friends and kinsfolk in the professions of medicine and law are all extolled in similar strains of hyperbolical eulogy. And as he pronounces his panegyrics, with an air of confidence, apparently arising from superior judgment, he misleads great numbers, and has actually raised to some degree of eminence a tribe of poor creatures, who, without puffing, would long ago have sunk in penury and oblivion.

But his puffing exertions are most ardently and laboriously displayed in the field of politics. He is not without hope of raising himself to some valuable post, when the party whom he puffs shall come into power.

'Was you at the House last night?' No; I went to see the play that you recommended. 'Well, you were, no doubt, admirably entertained; but yet, I wish you had been in the House. O, my God, Sir, I suppose there never was such a display of brilliancy since the world issued out of chaos. My friend Mr. —— was great indeed—astonishingly great—great beyond expression, beyond conception. No eloquence but his own can do justice to his stupendous powers. I look upon it, we have the three greatest *luminaries* now in the House, that the world ever saw, and all on one side; they have been called, indeed, through lack of better comparisons, the Demosthenes, the Cicero, and the Pericles of the age. But, my dear Sir, Demosthenes, Cicero, and Pericles, were not fit to hold a candle to Mr. ——, or Mr. ——, or my Lord ——. They were children and fools to them. I look upon it, eloquence in the hands of this glorious *triumvirate*, has reached the acmé of perfection. Upon my soul, nature and art are so combined in them, have wrought in them so finished a work, that they can go no farther; they have exhausted all the powers, and must rest and sleep for ages, before they can give birth to productions resembling, in the remotest degree, these great *luminaries.* They thunder, they lighten, they shake the whole nation like an earthquake, by their stupendous oratory. It was said of Plato, that if the gods were to converse with mortals, they would adopt his language. It might be more truly said of Mr. ——. O Chatham, Chatham, thou never hadst an idea of eloquence. If the *luminaries* could but come into power, how would the nation flourish! Such powers —are equal to the government of the universe; fit to wield the real thunder and lightning above; fit to rule the privy council of heaven, or rather to depose and usurp its dominion. The earth is unworthy of such *luminaries.* The generality want power of vision to bear their brilliancy. Therefore these men are not in office:—but, like roses, *blush unseen,* and waste their fragrance in the desert air.'

But as the puffer blows a prosperous gale on those whom he wishes to serve, however undeserving, so he breathes a foul pestilential blast on the fairest characters, and the richest desert, which are rising to fame and fortune without being likely to promote his interest, his vanity, his party, and his profession.

He studies the arts of detraction with as much attention as the arts of unmerited praise.

'Who is that scribbler whom you mention?' he cries, when he hears another praising a man of merit; 'I really never heard his name before. Has he written any thing? Bless me, I make a point of seeing every thing of any repute; but I never was fortunate enough to meet with Mr. —— (I beg your pardon; I forget the person's name you mentioned), Mr. ——'s Works. But I will inquire—I dare say I can get them in quires at the cheesemonger's.'

Such a one is a good preacher, says somebody. 'I really cannot speak to that point. I, for my part, was very drowsy; and, egad! all the people in the pew where I sat, who were decidedly the most intelligent in the church, were asleep, except my friend Professor ——, who must be acknowledged to be a good judge, and he was stuffing his pudding sleeves into his mouth to prevent a fit of laughter.'

A charming picture that of Sir Joshua's.—'La! la! The Knight grows old—breaks apace—indeed I never saw any thing to admire in his fugacious colours.'

Praise the physician who has saved your life, or the judge who has done you justice, and he lifts up his brows and exclaims: 'Dr. H. is an old woman,

Judge ——, another; Lord —— does not understand law—but may be a mighty good man for
aught I know.'

As to statesmen and senatorial orators, they are
all fools and knaves, but those of the party by
whom he hopes to be rewarded for puffing and
paragraphing with something more solid than empty
praise.

In dispensing both censure and applause, he has
no regard to truth, and the conviction of his own
mind; but has arrived at such depravity as to be
able to invent and propagate fictitious stories to
confirm his sentences of men and their conduct,
whether favourable or unfavourable. It is from
such men as he that *paragraphs in the public prints*
appear blackening or brightening individuals, for
interested or malicious purposes, without the least
attention to delicacy, justice, or veracity. The evil
has indeed been carried to such lengths as to have
almost become its own remedy; for the suspicions
of mankind are awakened by reiterated deception,
and credulity and malice, from having been often
and ridiculously duped, begin to learn distrust and
candour.

But the misfortune is, that just and merited praise
often loses all its effect by being confounded with
the hyperbolical and false encomiums of the puffer;
and that modesty and truth, unassuming, unpre-
tending, and rather diffident from the delicacy attending them, are either left unnoticed, or robbed of
all their honours by the bold and interested detractor. The cultivation of solid worth is thus
discouraged; and a study of the mean arts of securing the rewards of virtue without possessing its
intrinsic value, promoted. Private happiness is thus
diminished among those who deserve to enjoy it unmolested; and the public welfare injured by dis-

couraging virtuous and laborious exertion. Puffers ought therefore to be exposed, to be avoided as nuisances to society, and viewed with as much suspicion, as sharpers, swindlers, gamesters, and the whole fraternity of unprincipled adventurers.

Immoderate praise is, indeed, become very suspicious; and a man of sense is as much upon his guard against its effect on his mind, as against the advertisements of quack-doctors, and the *particulars* of auctioneers. He argues that there must be something ugly that requires so much gilding to cover it; something rotten, or blemished, where the thing recommended cannot be obtruded on notice without a profusion of paint and varnish.

It is diverting to consider how highly every little excellence is praised in the present age, by those who are interested in forcing it into celebrity. As the orator of the hammer denominates a cit's country-box, a villa and a mansion; a cistern, a reservoir; a horse-pond, a canal; a ditch, a trout-stream; a grass-plot, ten feet by twelve, a paddock: so a little sprig of divinity is equalled, in the praises of the puffer, to a Tillotson; a young practitioner, that has hardly walked the hospital, to a Boerhaave; a pragmatical pleader, as soon as he has thrown a tie-wig over his toupee, to a Coke or a Littleton; a petty catgut-scraper, to an Apollo; a canvas-spoiler, to an Apelles; a rhymer, to a Pope; a builder of a messuage, two rooms on a floor, to a Wren. Every hill is brought low by him, and every valley exalted.

Such eulogies are lavished on mediocrity, or even demerit, as were never given, in their lifetime at least, to Lord Chancellor Bacon, to Sir Isaac Newton, to Shakspeare, to Milton, to Handel, to all whom Fame has justly placed in the most honourables niches of her temple. It seems to be an adopted maxim in the present age, that if glory come not till after death, it comes too late. And the goddess Fame seems to attend to it judiciously; for as she gives so much during the lives of her votaries, she withholds all memory of most of them immediately on their decease.

Upon the whole, it may be said with truth, that praise, from its prostitution, is in many cases become satire, and satire an honour; and that censure or neglect is now, in a variety of instances, creditable, for it proves that the man to whom it is shewn, has left his merit to stand or fall, as it might be able of itself; and in the honesty of an upright and ingenuous spirit, has scorned to use sinister or collusive arts to repel the weapons of envy and malice.

END OF VOL. XLII.

Printed by J. F. DOVE, St. John's Square.